A Cloistered World

Abbeys and Priories of North-Eastern England

A Cloistered World

Abbeys and Priories of North-Eastern England

Glen Lyndon Dodds

Albion
Press

Albion Press
40 Park Parade Roker Sunderland Tyne & Wear
ISBN 978 0 9525122 8 8

Cover photograph: Rievaulx Abbey
Back cover photograph: Jervaulx Abbey
Title page photograph: Durham Cathedral cloister

Typeset and designed by UpStyle Book Design
www.upstyle.co.uk
Printed and bound in Great Britain by
the MPG Books Group, Bodmin and King's Lynn

CONTENTS

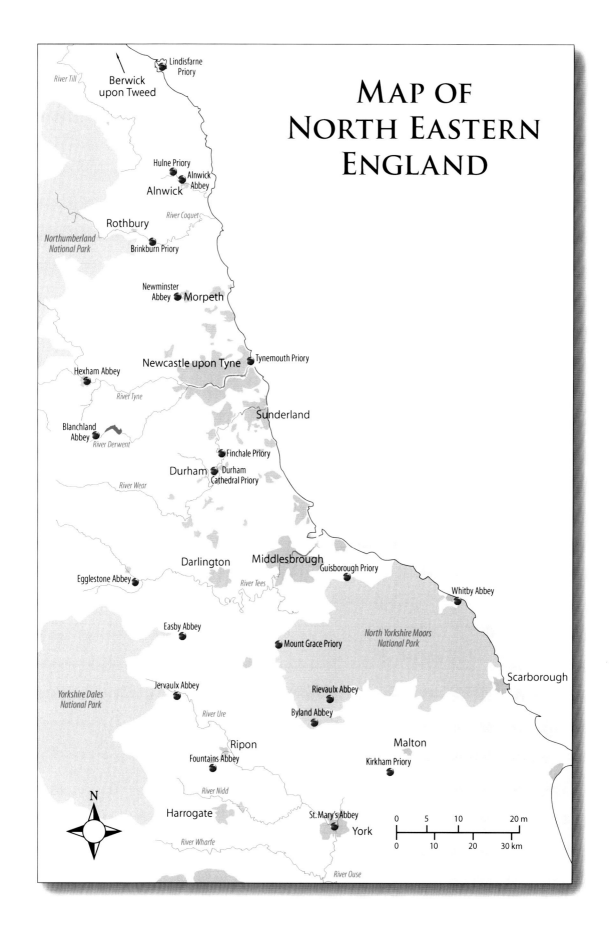

MAP OF NORTH EASTERN ENGLAND

River Till

Lindisfarne Priory

Berwick upon Tweed

Hulne Priory
Alnwick Abbey
Alnwick

Rothbury

River Coquet

Northumberland National Park

Brinkburn Priory

Newminster Abbey ● Morpeth

Hexham Abbey

Newcastle upon Tyne ● Tynemouth Priory

River Tyne

Blanchland Abbey
River Derwent

Sunderland

Finchale Priory

Durham ● Durham Cathedral Priory

River Wear

Darlington

Middlesbrough

Guisborough Priory

Whitby Abbey

Egglestone Abbey

River Tees

Easby Abbey

North Yorkshire Moors National Park

Mount Grace Priory

Scarborough

Jervaulx Abbey

Yorkshire Dales National Park

River Ure

Rievaulx Abbey

Byland Abbey

Ripon

Malton

Fountains Abbey

Kirkham Priory

River Nidd

Harrogate

N

St. Mary's Abbey
York

River Wharfe

| 0 | 5 | 10 | 20 m |
| 0 | 10 | 20 | 30 km |

River Ouse

RELIGIOUS HOUSES IN NORTH-EASTERN ENGLAND DURING THE MIDDLE AGES

Monasticism was an important facet of medieval Christendom, but at the time of the Norman Conquest no monasteries lay in north-eastern England. However, they had existed in the days of the Anglo-Saxon kingdom of Northumbria and included renowned communities such as Wearmouth and Jarrow, founded in the late 7th century. Subsequent Viking activity brought monastic life in the region to an end, and it was only in the late 11th century, by which time England had come under Norman rule, that monasteries reappeared. This process was in full swing during the 12th century, when numerous religious houses were founded.

In addition to genuine piety, founders of religious communities were motivated by other considerations. By establishing monasteries, members of the upper classes could for example gain additional prestige in society and ensure that they would be remembered by future generations.

The monastic world was not uniform. For one thing, some of the religious houses in the region belonged to the Benedictine Order. In Italy, in the 6th century, St Benedict had devised a set of highly influential instructions for a monastery that he founded at Monte Cassino. These regulations became known as the Benedictine Rule. Benedictine monks had to obey vows of lifelong personal poverty and chastity. They were also required to divide their lives into three parts—in addition to celebrating Mass, on a daily basis they were to observe the Canonical Hours (a practice that required seven acts of corporate worship, including services during the night); were to engage in reading and meditation of a spiritual nature; and do manual labour. By the Middle Ages however, the latter requirement had died away.

The same basic framework of liturgy laid down by Benedict was followed by other monastic bodies, including the Cistercian Order. The Cistercians (whose earliest monastery was established at Cîteaux in France in 1098) were very austere. Also known as the White Monks because they wore undyed or white habits, Cistercians embraced poverty with fervour. The early Cistercians favoured settling on uncultivated terrain upon which they could live a frugal, self-supporting existence. Furthermore they rejected items such as undershirts, breeches and fur-lined boots (which must have been sorely missed in northern climes during harsh weather) and their places of worship had less ornament than was the norm.

The Cistercians were organised as a family tree and annual inspections of daughter houses were conducted by the abbot of the parent house. For example, Roche Abbey in southern Yorkshire was founded by monks from Newminster in Northumberland and was therefore visited by Newminster's abbot. In turn, Newminster received visitations from the abbot of its own parent house, Fountains.

Cistercian communities also included lay brothers, a subordinate group who

The great cloister at Mount Grace Priory

wore brown habits. These lived apart from the monks and followed a less rigorous programme of worship. They performed many essential tasks on behalf of the monks such as growing their food and tending flocks and herds. Other monastic orders followed suit and had lay brothers of their own, as was true for example of the Carthusian Order.

The Carthusians, whose first community was established near Grenoble in France, were governed by a set of regulations drawn up in the early 12th century. To a marked degree, Carthusian monks shunned contact with the outside world. They were vowed to silence—speech was only permitted when deemed essential or on occasions such as feast days—and were taught that physical poverty enhanced their spiritual wealth. Hence they wore the roughest possible hair shirts and additional clothing was scanty, coarse and undyed. The diet was likewise extremely spartan. Three days a week they subsisted on water and bread made from unbolted flour. Meagre rations of fish, cheese, eggs and vegetables were allowed on the other days. In addition, Carthusians did not share the communal life practised by other monastic orders. They gathered in the priory church for High Mass and only two Canonical Hours, Matins and Vespers. The other Hours were observed in their respective cells, located around a great cloister, where they spent the bulk of their time alone, worshipping, reading, meditating and working.

Religious houses also included communities of Augustinian and Premonstratensian canons. In contrast to monks, they were not tonsured, but their lives were based on the monastic model.

Alternatively known as the Black Canons, on account of their black robes, Augustinians lived by a rule based on the writings and letters of an early 5th century bishop, St Augustine of Hippo and the first Augustinian houses in England were founded in the early 12th century.

The Augustinians were less austere than other orders. For example, the daily routine of worship, although still demanding, was not as time consuming. Food and drink were also less restricted. There was also more freedom to converse and to go beyond the bounds of the monastery into the world at large and Augustinians could minister in parish churches granted to their respective houses.

Premonstratensians, who reached England in the mid 12th century, also observed the Rule of St Augustine and could serve a pastoral role in churches owned by their abbeys. Known as the White Canons on account of their habits of undyed woollen cloth, Premonstratensians were austere and strongly influenced by the Cistercians, some of whose regulations they adopted.

To a lesser degree, other canons—members of the Gilbertine Order founded in the 12th century—likewise had a presence in the region. They had houses in Yorkshire at Malton and St Andrew's, York. Gilbertine canons likewise followed the Rule of St Augustine.

Religious houses, of course, also included nunneries. In the vast majority of cases these were very poorly endowed establishments founded in the 12th century. Yorkshire contained over 20 female monasteries. Several lay in the north-eastern part of the county and included St Clement's, a Benedictine community located just outside the city walls of York. It was founded by Archbishop Thurstan in or shortly after 1125 and was the first nunnery established in Yorkshire. Only one nunnery existed in County Durham—Neasham, a Benedictine priory first mentioned in 1156 and located at Hurworth-on-Tees. Four nunneries lay in Northumberland and the most important of these was an early 12th century foundation, St Bartholomew's, a Benedictine community in Newcastle upon Tyne.

The 13th century witnessed the arrival of new religious orders, namely those of the friars—Friar Tuck, who appears in Robin Hood films set in the 1190s, is an anachronism. The most important orders were the Dominican, also known as the Black Friars, and the Franciscan or Grey Friars: both were founded in the early years of the 13th century, the former by St Dominic of Osma, the latter by St Francis of Assisi.

Although their houses closely resembled monasteries, friars (in contrast to religious communities that lived by the monastic model) lived by begging and were committed to preaching. Thus, far from trying to cut themselves off from the world, they generally preferred to establish themselves in urban areas. Hence, in addition to preaching in the friary church, friars did so in the market place and on

The ruins of Guyzance nunnery in Northumberland

the street corner. Occasionally, they were invited to preach in parish churches and cathedrals.

In Yorkshire, the first order of friars to make a mark were the Dominicans, who set up a friary at York in 1227. They were followed by the Franciscans and others. Indeed, in all, six friaries were established in the city though two proved short-lived. In County Durham, friars made less headway. They had a strong presence at Hartlepool, where a Franciscan friary was established on the headland in the 13th century by the aristocratic Bruce family, but a Franciscan community at Durham City proved a brief affair. In Northumberland, friaries were more numerous. From the 1230s onward they were created in various towns, including Berwick upon Tweed (at this date a Scottish burgh) and Newcastle upon Tyne. At Newcastle, all five orders of friars were represented and the same was true of Berwick.

Abbeys and priories lay in precincts that varied considerably in size, but could be as large as approximately 100 acres (40.5 hectares). Those of poor communities were defined by banks, ditches etc., but wealthier monasteries were enclosed by stone walls (those of St Mary's Abbey, York, had battlements) with imposing gatehouses.

Precincts not only encompassed a church, cloister, and buildings to accommodate the community, but structures such as guesthouses. Normally, they also contained buildings associated with industrial and agricultural activity. Gardens, fishponds, orchards and meadowland could also be found within their boundaries.

The availability of suitable building materials was one of the prime factors in determining the location of a monastery. An adequate supply of water, and the provision of good drainage, was also vital. Consequently, religious houses were often located beside streams or rivers, with buildings such as lavatories laid out to take into account the flow of water through the precinct.

The church, the largest and most important edifice, was usually cruciform in plan and the western arm, the nave, was sometimes used entirely or in part by laity. In male establishments, the cloister usually lay against the south side of the nave whereas at nunneries it was often located north of the nave. The cloister was an open space, often square in plan, enclosed by covered walks or alleys running around the inner side of buildings overlooking the cloister. The cloister walks were spaces where the monks, canons and so on, engaged in various activities such as writing, studying and copying manuscripts.

The gatehouse at Easby Abbey

Every monastery possessed a network of estates. Often the bulk of the land lay within the vicinity of the house, but property could also lie many miles away. For example, Fountains had holdings near Teesmouth, and in the parish of Kirby Wiske in the Vale of York, whereas Whitby's more distant possessions included property at Yarm and Thornaby-on-Tees. For its part, Durham Cathedral Priory held land well to the north, in an outlying part of the bishopric of Durham known as Norhamshire located beside the River Tweed. Some other property of the same monastery was also far-flung.

Granges formed part of the monastic landscape. Newminster is a case in point. At property located miles from the abbey, such as at Ritton, Ulgham and Kidland, the monks established granges to exploit its resources. Each grange had a chapel, dormitory and refectory as well as farm buildings. For much of the monastery's history, the granges were each manned by lay brothers under the supervision of a monk who was also a priest and they would all return to Newminster periodically for major Church festivals.

Granges could have various functions. Some were primarily involved in sheep farming and were often located in upland areas—Guisborough, for example, had the majority of its sheep granges in Eskdale. Others were primarily involved in industrial activity or arable farming.

Arable farming was certainly an important facet of monastic economies. For instance, the extremely fertile lands forming the northern and southern sides of the Vale of Pickering were heavily exploited by houses like Byland and Rievaulx. Arable farming also occurred in the less favourable central part of the vale—where much of the terrain was more suited to pastoralism—and in some cases did so on reclaimed marshland. Rievaulx is a case in point. It commenced worthwhile reclamation work there in the mid 12th century.

Sheep featured prominently in monastic economies for they provided milk, cheese, manure, mutton and, above all, wool. The foremost sheep farmers were the Cistercians—their houses at Rievaulx and Jervaulx, for example, were major exporters and noted for the quality of the fleeces they produced. Nevertheless, the other orders also had large flocks. In the mid 15th century, for instance, Durham Cathedral Priory, a Benedictine house, operated a farm at Saltholme on Teesside

Jervaulx Abbey viewed from the west

devoted to sheep, where the salt-marshes produced a grass that was very good for the fleece. Even small nunneries were involved in the wool trade, as was true for example of Rosedale, a remote Cistercian priory in the heart of the North York Moors, whose flock was around 2000 strong in 1308.

Fisheries were also important as a source of food and revenue. Rievaulx illustrates the point. Bryan Waites comments that the abbey 'held a very great interest in the Tees fisheries along almost the whole lower course of the river ....The monks, for instance, had the entire fishery of Newsham and no one else was to fish there but them.'

In addition, monasteries obtained significant revenue from churches in their possession, income derived, for example, from tithes and produce of glebe lands. In some cases, churches were part of the initial endowment, as was true of Guisborough, whose founder gave the priory 10 churches.

Monasteries also engaged in industrial activity. Coal was mined at various places on land belonging to Tynemouth Priory, such as Elswick and Marden, and a rental drawn up in 1292 estimated that annual revenue from this source exceeded £3. In 1339, moreover, Durham acquired a pit at Ferryhill for £22, and subsequently senior monks visited the site to inspect the workings. The same monastery had other coal mining interests in the vicinity and elsewhere.

A number of religious houses also engaged in mining ironstone and working iron. Byland ranked among them, for it exploited ironstone deposits near Wakefield. Guisborough and Fountains are other examples. The former had important iron works in Eskdale and its tributary valleys (most notably Glaisdale) whereas Fountains had iron-smelting forges at Aldborough near Ripon and on a grange at Bradley in the vicinity of Huddersfield.

As noted above, Fountains also possessed property in the Teesmouth area, whose tidal flats were one of the foremost locations of saltmaking in medieval England, and other houses with interests in the same neighbourhood included Byland, Guisborough and Rievaulx. For its part, Durham likewise obtained salt (and revenue from salt pans) from the villages of Cowpen and Greatham in the same area, as well as further up the coast at, for example, Sunderland where it possessed a salt pan. Alnwick, Newminster and Tynemouth were among religious houses that also possessed salt pans.

Military conflict sometimes caused major disruption, especially during the Wars of Scottish Independence and in the summer of 1314—following the English defeat at Bannockburn—Scots were at large in Northumberland and County Durham. Indeed, they crossed the Tees into Yorkshire and ventured beyond Richmond. Other incursions followed. In 1316, for example, the estates of Whitby Abbey had been so badly damaged by enemy activity that the abbot was compelled to obtain corn and other supplies from elsewhere.

Consequently, monastic houses throughout the region were adversely affected. Durham is a case in point. For instance, the revenue received from one of its officials, the proctor of Norham, plummeted. In the years building up to 1314, the proctor's

The west towers of Durham Cathedral

income (obtained from the parish of Norham and a substantial part of the neigh-bouring parish of Holy Island), usually totalled £400 or so per annum but thereafter it fell steeply. In 1318–19 the figure raised was pathetic; approximately £9!

Further misery was wrought by the Black Death. It struck the region in the spring of 1349 and claimed numerous lives—Byland and Rievaulx had to appoint new abbots that year—and, in addition to members of the religious orders, the pesti-lence inevitably also killed off tenants belonging to the region's monasteries, as was true on 28 townships belonging to Durham where, on average, over 50 per cent of the tenants perished.

Monastic life in this region, and nationally, ceased during the Dissolution of the Monasteries in the reign of Henry VIII. The closure of religious houses occurred in the years 1536–40 after the Reformation Parliament passed legislation that broke England away from Rome.

Initially, Henry's financially hard-pressed government moved against the smaller houses, those with annual incomes of less than £200, though a number of these were permitted to continue in existence. Some of Henry's subjects resented the closure of monasteries and participated in an unsuccessful rebellion known as the Pilgrimage of Grace that engulfed much of northern England in 1536. Following the rising, the programme of closure continued and within the next few years all the remaining monasteries were suppressed and their assets taken into the hands of the Crown.

Many members of the dissolved houses were awarded annual pensions related to the wealth of their respective monastery. In addition, members of some of the religious houses who had served at parish churches continued to do so following the Dissolution. In such a role, they were also joined by fellow former brethren and some ex-friars who were absorbed into the parochial system. In Northumberland, for example, Edward Hutton, a former canon of Brinkburn, served as Vicar of Felton until 1547 when a former canon of Alnwick stepped into his shoes.

The fate of the region's religious houses since the Dissolution has varied considerably. In some cases, such as Newminster, virtually nothing remains standing. On the other hand, at other sites like Fountains and Rievaulx, far more has survived and the visitor can see imposing ruins. Moreover, in some instances—Durham Cathedral is the most spectacular example—the monastic church has survived and still serves as a place of worship.

ALNWICK ABBEY

Alnwick Abbey was founded in 1147 as a house for Premonstratensian canons by Eustace fitzJohn, who was described by the chronicler William of Newburgh as a 'great man...among the chief English nobles, most eminent in his wealth and wisdom.' The canons who formed the first community, came from Newhouse in Lincolnshire, and Alnwick was the second Premonstratensian monastery established in England.

Eustace, who had acquired the barony of Alnwick through marriage, endowed the abbey with the church of Lesbury and its chapels of Houghton, Alnmouth and Alnwick. The endowment also included, among other things, the vill of Wycliffe and all the tithes of fitzJohn's fisheries, and those of such stags, does and swine 'as my dogs may catch by my will.'

Eustace, who also founded the Gilbertine priories of Malton and Watton in Yorkshire, died campaigning with Henry II in Wales in 1157. His son and successor, William, was also a benefactor of the abbey for he gave the canons the churches of Alnham, Chatton and Chillingham. He became a Premonstratensian canon and, following his death in 1184, was laid to rest before the door of the chapter house, the first of several lords of Alnwick buried in the abbey.

Meanwhile, in the early 1150s, canons from Alnwick had crossed the River Tweed to form the nucleus of a new Premonstratensian house at Dryburgh in Berwickshire—a monastery founded by a member of the Scottish court—and the first and most important Premonstratensian house in that kingdom.

Heads of monastic houses were sometimes removed from office and this fate befell Abbot Adam of Alnwick. For one reason or another, he was deposed on 9 December 1208.

Later in the 13th century, when the lord of Alnwick, John de Vescy, died in Gascony in 1287 the abbot had his bones brought back to Northumberland. On 10 February 1288, they were buried in the abbey church 'with great honour.'

The Abbot of Alnwick was one of 13 heads of Premonstratensian communities whom Edward I summoned to the parliament of Carlisle in January 1307. In the event, the abbot did not attend and sent a proctor to do so instead.

The early 14th century was a troubled time in the region, largely as a result of Anglo-Scottish warfare and in 1313 Richard Kellaw, the Bishop of Durham (within whose vast diocese Alnwick lay), augmented the abbey's resources by granting the canons the united benefices of Wooler and Fenton. In that year, some of the canons at Alnwick were termed 'bishop's canons' and their special assignment was to pray for the soul of the Bishop of Durham and the patrons of the house.

Premonstratensian canons were permitted to serve a pastoral role, and in 1331 Alnwick sought permission from the Bishop of Durham to replace secular clergy with its own canons at three of the monastery's churches: Alnham, Shilbottle and Lesbury.

In 1376, Abbot Walter of Hepscott is reported by the chronicler of Alnwick Abbey to have entertained 'our noble patron Henry...lord Percy' and 13 knights to dinner in the refectory, while 1,020 of the abbeys 'parishioners' of all ages and the commons of the country ate in the cloister. Henry Percy's great-grandfather had acquired the barony of Alnwick in 1309, and Henry himself became the first Earl of Northumberland the year after he was entertained by Hepscott.

Several generations later, in 1519, the fifth Earl of Northumberland agreed to provide 10 marks a year 'for the payment of a pedagogue or master to read and teach Grammar and Philosophy to the canons and brethren of Alnwick.'

Alnwick Abbey was suppressed in 1539.

Description

The remains of Alnwick Abbey are located on the north side of the River Aln on the outskirts of the town of Alnwick. The only building that still stands is the gatehouse, which was built in the late 14th century. It is a substantial two-storey rectangular structure, with a tunnel-vaulted entrance passage. Boldly projecting corner turrets with embattled parapets rise higher than the rest of the building, which also has battlements.

The gatehouse lies in Hulne Park, which belongs to the Duke of Northumberland and is usually open to the general public.

Alnwick Abbey's imposing gatehouse

BLACKFRIARS, NEWCASTLE

Newcastle's Dominican friary was located in the northwest sector of the medieval town and was founded, by the close of the 1230s at the latest, by a prosperous merchant named Sir Peter Scot. In addition to the seven acres (almost three hectares) or so of ground where the friary lay, Newcastle's Black Friars, as members of the Dominican Order were also known, had two gardens and four small closes that provided a meagre income.

The Dominican Order kept an eye on its religious houses and at times priors who erred seriously were removed from office. This fate befell Newcastle's prior in 1250. He was found guilty of spending too much money on construction work—fabric dating from this period can still be seen at the site, located on Friars Street—and of compelling the friars to live on inadequate rations because of the heavy debts incurred.

Friaries sometimes entertained important visitors, and this was certainly true of Newcastle's Dominican community. In the 14th century, for example, the friars accommodated royalty on more than one occasion. Indeed, in June 1334, England's martial young king Edward III and his Scottish counterpart, Edward Balliol, were

A view across the site of the demolished church towards the chapter house (left) and other buildings

present with their retinues. In the friary church, Balliol—who had secured the Scottish throne with Edward III's support—gave his homage to England's sovereign.

On 10 January 1539, Blackfriars was shut down and the property passed into royal hands.

Description

The church of the friary no longer survives. It was demolished in the 16th century and lay on the north side of the site—laity used to gather in the nave to hear the friars preach.

To the south of the church, was a cloister enclosed by the church and by two-storey ranges of buildings. The claustral ranges still stand, albeit subject to various alterations in more recent times. The chapter house was the main room in the east range. Some of the present structure is Victorian, but the west wall dates from the late 13th century and has an arched doorway, flanked by two windows, one of which is a restoration. The rest of the east range likewise contains medieval and Victorian fabric. The south range (largely post-medieval) originally contained the refectory, whereas the west range, which included the lavatorium, partly served as a guesthouse.

There is no entrance fee.

BLANCHLAND ABBEY

The founder of Blanchland Abbey was a Northumbrian baron named Walter de Bolbec, who lived at Styford a few miles southeast of Corbridge and was lord of the barony of Bolbec. He is usually identified as Walter III, but was in reality Walter de Bolbec II, the son of the man to whom Henry I had granted the barony.

Blanchland Abbey lies in Northumberland and is located in the picturesque valley of the River Derwent on the border between Northumberland and County Durham, and was founded in 1165 as a house for Premonstratensian canons. The first canons came from Croxton Abbey in Leicestershire and the first abbot, Alan, had previously served as Abbot of Croxton.

Walter de Bolbec granted the new monastery land on the north side of the Derwent upon which to build the abbey. Moreover, among other things, he endowed the small monastic community with the church of Kirkharle and that of St Andrew, Bywell, together with the latter's three dependent chapels—Styford, Apperley and Shotley. Although his sons Walter III and Hugh (his successor) added to the monastery's property, Blanchland was never well endowed.

Evidently, for part of its history Blanchland was viewed as a daughter house of

The church at Blanchland

Looking along the north transept towards the base of the tower

Newhouse in Lincolnshire, the oldest Premonstratensian Abbey in England. Blanch-land had been established with the advice of the Abbot of Newhouse and, as noted, the first canons came from Croxton, a daughter of Newhouse. Hence, as H.M. Colvin comments, 'father abbots were inclined to assume jurisdiction over their daughter-houses' offspring in cases where the new foundation had taken place under their own direction.' By the early 14th century however, Blanchland was viewed as a daughter house of Croxton.

During this period, owing to the negligent rule of the abbot, the fortunes of the abbey were at a very low ebb. News of this reached France. In 1314 the Abbot of Prémontré called upon Richard Kellaw, the Bishop of Durham, to sequestrate within his diocese all the monastery's sources of spiritual revenue—income derived from its churches. The bishop put the request into effect, until the election of a new abbot was announced.

In 1327, Blanchland suffered at the hands of Scottish raiders and thus claimed, in a petition to Edward III and his council, that the abbey had incurred the loss of 40 acres of wheat and rye, 100 acres of oats, 100 acres of hay and 500 sheep. As a result, food worth 20 marks was despatched to Blanchland from a royal depot at Newcastle. On this point, Richard Lomas comments: 'The interesting aspect of this petition was that the canons attached blame not only to the Scots, but also to English government purveyors who were legally entitled to take goods on the promise of future payment.'

Blanchland Abbey was closed in 1540 during the Dissolution of the Monasteries.

Description

A substantial amount of the abbey church still survives. It was retained when the church, which had become ruinous, was partly rebuilt in the mid 18th century. The medieval work mostly dates from the 13th century and includes a tower adjoining the north side of the north transept—no south transept was ever built. The tower is of three stages: the lower two were erected in the 13th century whereas the upper-most dates from the mid 14th century. Other medieval fabric includes the chancel, although the east end was rebuilt in 1881. The nave has not survived—its former south wall now separates the churchyard from the garden of a neighbouring hotel.

The hotel is the enchanting Lord Crewe Arms, which occupies the west range of claustral buildings. Just across the road, lies a sturdy 15th century monastic gate-house whose ground floor contains the village post office.

BRINKBURN PRIORY

B rinkburn Priory lies in a lovely setting beside a loop of the River Coquet deep in Northumberland, and was founded in, or shortly before, 1135 by William de Bertram, lord of Mitford.

Brinkburn was an Augustinian house, and the first canons likely came from Pentney Priory in Norfolk. Brinkburn was never wealthy and little is known of its history. In around 1322, by which time Northumberland had suffered from Scottish raids and natural disasters, the prior and canons petitioned Edward II in the hope of gaining financial assistance in view of losses they had sustained.

During the 14th century, the canons built a chamber above the aisle of the nave. Another addition to the church, and possibly contemporaneous with the chamber, was a room erected above the chancel. Their function is uncertain.

Brinkburn Priory survived until 1536 when it was closed during the Dissolution of the Monasteries. Thereafter, the church remained in use as a place of worship serving local people: laity had already had access to the west part of the nave. The building remained in a decent condition until the end of the 16th century, but then began to decay: the roof collapsed during the 17th century and regular services came to an end in 1683.

In the mid 19th century, the church was restored by Cadogan Hodgson Cadogan, who owned Brinkburn. Among other things, the collapsed southwest angle of the nave, the most extensively damaged part of the fabric, was rebuilt, and the chambers erected over the aisle of the nave and the chancel were removed.

Description

The church, a fine example of late northern Transitional architecture, is entered through a doorway, enriched with Norman ornament, located in a gabled projection on the north side of the nave. The church was probably commenced around 1190 and construction continued into the early decades of the following century.

The nave has a north aisle, whose arcade has octagonal piers. East of the nave lies the crossing, beneath a low tower. Both transepts have a rib-vaulted east aisle. The aisles formerly had wooden screens—the beam holes survive—and served as chapels. In the north transept is a large wooden sculpture, *The Risen Christ*, a modern work by Fenwick Lawson. The south transept contains an organ built in 1868 by William Hill, possibly the most important English organ-maker of the 19th century.

In the chancel, a doorway (now blocked) was inserted when a sacristy was built against the north side of the chancel. Although nearly all of the floor tiles in the church date from the 19th century, some of those beneath the high altar are medieval. The east wall of the chancel is the most imposing of the church and has three tiers of windows; two comprise lancets whereas the highest has smaller, round-headed, windows.

The priory church (right) and manor house

In the west wall of the south transept, a doorway opens to the site of the former cloister. Only vestiges of the east claustral range survive, and nothing of the west range, if indeed one was ever built. On the other hand, much of the south range, which contained the canons' refectory, has been incorporated within a manor house, an empty shell open to visitors.

Brinkburn Priory is now in the care of English Heritage.

BYLAND ABBEY

Byland, one of the greatest Cistercian monasteries in Britain, was located on the fringe of the North York Moors and had a troubled start. The community was formed in the mid 1130s when Furness, a Savigniac abbey in the North West, sent monks under an abbot named Gerold to found a monastery at Calder in present day Cumbria. However, in 1137 or the following year, the fledgling monastery was destroyed by Scottish raiders. Hence the monks abandoned the site, and soon set off eastward to seek the help of Archbishop Thurstan of York. As a result, a young aristocrat named Roger de Mowbray provided the monks with a place to stay at Hood near Thirsk in Yorkshire.

Abbot Gerold died in 1142 and was succeeded by a member of the community called Roger. As Hood was constricted and unsuitable for expansion, the new abbot soon moved the abbey north to a larger site at Byland in Ryedale. But there was a fly in the ointment. Old Byland (as it has since become known) was close to Rievaulx Abbey, a Cistercian house. According to a history written in 1197 by Roger's successor, the communities could hear each other's bells 'which was not fitting and could by no means be endured.'

In 1147, therefore, the monks moved southward to Stocking, and built a small monastery. In the same year, the Savigniac Order was absorbed by Cîteaux and so the house became Cistercian.

While at Stocking, the community acquired a tract of waste and marshy ground not far to the east, one that the monks believed would make a better site. Therefore, they 'began manfully to root out the woods, and by long and wide ditches to draw off the abundance of water from the marshes; and when dry land appeared they prepared for themselves an ample, fitting and worthy site in the eastern part of that land.' Building operations then commenced. By 1177 the new monastery, located at the present site, was habitable and the community moved to its new home.

Work on constructing a vast church was still in progress, but was completed by the close of the century. The finished building, 330ft (100m) long and 140ft (43m) across the transepts, was the largest Cistercian place of worship in Britain at the time, bigger than many contemporary cathedrals. Moreover, Stuart Harrison comments that its 'place in the development of Gothic architecture cannot be over-emphasised, as it was one of the first buildings in the north fully to break away from the Romanesque tradition.'

During Roger's abbacy (1142–96), the house grew very wealthy and enjoyed its greatest period, although the size of the community is unknown. Byland was still prominent in 1231 when it was stipulated that the number of monks should not exceed 80 and that the recruitment of lay brothers should cease until their number was under 160.

The west front of the church

In 1322, the monastery was plundered by the Scots. In addition, the abbey was evidently badly affected by the subsequent Black Death, and in 1381 the community only numbered 11 monks and three lay brothers. There were 26 monks, including the abbot, when Byland was surrendered into royal hands on 30 November 1538.

Description

The ruins are dominated by the church's impressive west front, completed around 1195. It is the finest surviving feature of the abbey and was the last part of the church to be erected. Above a richly moulded central doorway, and a tier of tall lancets, are the remains of a magnificent rose window, 26ft (8m) in diameter, the first of such scale in England.

The church comprised an aisled nave; a crossing surmounted by a low tower; transepts with west and east aisles; and a chancel that terminated in a row of five chapels. The main parts of the church had timber barrel-vaults. Apparently, in the 1230s the entire building was provided with tiled floors—some arranged to form complex geometrical patterns—and important survivals of this can be seen in the east aisle of the south transept.

Buildings ranged around the cloister, one of the largest in the country, all date from c.1155–1177. The east range conforms to the normal Cistercian pattern and included a rib-vaulted chapter house. Beyond the chapter house, are the remains, respectively, of the parlour; a passage through the range that led eastward to the monks' latrine block; the day stairs to the dormitory (which occupied the entire upper floor) and, occupying the southern end of the range, the largest ground floor room. The latter, originally served as a place where monks engaged in manual work and where tools were stored.

The monks' latrine block was built on an east-west axis and had a great drain down the centre, screened by walls. Running water removed effluent discharged into the drain, from a row of latrines at first floor level. The water that flushed this, and

Tiles and arcading in the chancel

A general view of the extensive ruins

other drains at Byland, came from a large dam constructed north of the church. In the early years of the 13th century, the latrine block was replaced by one erected on a north-south axis against its east end.

Further to the south, are the low remnants of the abbot's lodging, largely 13th century and later. A short distance to the west of the abbot's residence, stand remains of the meat kitchen, a small 15th century room. Where the meat was consumed is uncertain— regulations decreed that it could not be eaten in the normal refectory.

The south range included the monks' warming house and a kitchen where vegetarian meals were prepared, but the main part of the range comprised a refectory that projected southward and was built over a vaulted undercroft, an unusual feature for a Cistercian house.

The west range, the earliest part of the abbey, was completed by around 1165. In the 15th century, however, the west wall was reinforced by the provision of flying buttresses. The ground floor partly housed the lay brothers' dining hall. The upper floor served as their dormitory. In the latter years of Byland (by which time lay brothers had ceased to be members of the community) the range may have been used as a granary.

Finally, running eastward from the south end of the west range was the lay brothers' latrine block. This linked up with the monks' refectory, and the space to the north formed the lay brothers' cloister.

Byland Abbey is in the care of English Heritage.

DURHAM CATHEDRAL PRIORY

The Benedictine priory at Durham, one of England's leading monastic houses, stood on a peninsula formed by a loop of the River Wear and lay within the walls of Durham Castle. Although monastic life at the site has long ceased, the cathedral and claustral buildings survive and attract hundreds of thousands of visitors annually. Indeed, Durham Cathedral is one of the most celebrated buildings in the world.

Work on this magnificent church began under William de St Calais, who became Bishop of Durham in 1080. Viking raids during the 9th century had ended monastic life in the region. St Calais' predecessor, Walcher of Lorraine, wished to revive monasticism and had settled small groups of monks from the South and Midlands at Wearmouth and Jarrow. He also planned to found a Benedictine house at Durham, where secular clergy served a Saxon cathedral, 'the White Church.' However, he was murdered before he brought the scheme into being.

William de St Calais shared Walcher's desire. Hence in 1083 he removed the secular clergy—all but one had refused to take monastic vows—and transferred the monks at Wearmouth and Jarrow to Durham to form the nucleus of Durham Priory. The first prior was an Englishman, Aldwin of Winchcombe. He was responsible for the administration of the priory, whereas the bishop was its titular head.

In 1093, work on an imposing new cathedral began. It did so a year after St Calais had ordered the demolition of the Saxon church, which evidently lay just to the south of the site chosen for its replacement. Presumably, at least part of the Saxon building was retained until services could be held in the Norman cathedral.

Construction work proceeded from east to west, in line with normal practice, and by 1104 had advanced sufficiently for the reportedly uncorrupt body of St Cuthbert (d. 687) to be placed in a magnificent shrine just behind the high altar. However, most of the cathedral still needed to be built. By the time Geoffrey Rufus was appointed to the bishopric in 1133, construction work had to all intents and purposes just finished. Although additions have been made to the church, it is nevertheless the least altered Norman cathedral in England.

Over the years the cathedral had many visitors. These included countless pilgrims, intent on visiting the shrine of St Cuthbert, the North's premier saint, and the shrine, located at the east end of the church, was a source of great prestige and wealth for the monks. Women, however, were not allowed to approach the shrine for St Cuthbert gained a posthumous reputation for misogyny. Towards the west end of the nave, a marble line in the floor marks the spot beyond which they could not pass.

At the beginning of the 14th century, the peace of the monastery was disrupted in dramatic style when Bishop Antony Bek clashed with the prior, Richard Hoton. In

The cathedral (from the southwest) rising majestically over the River Wear

mid 1300 the angry bishop commenced a blockade of the priory and proceeded to cut off its main water supply. In short, the bishop was hell-bent on installing a new prior, so much so that on 21 August one of Bek's lieutenants, the constable of Durham Castle, at the head of armed men, forced his way into the monastery. Boldly, in a moment of high drama in the cathedral, Hoton refused to leave the prior's stall. He was not alone. Forty-six of his monks stubbornly remained in their stalls as well and thus experienced hunger and discomfort. Hoton and his men had to relieve themselves in the cathedral, 'which was an unheard of action by Christians up to that time.' Eventually, the monks submitted. But Hoton remained where he was until 24 August when he was dragged from his stall and imprisoned, whereupon Bek's choice as Hoton's replacement (who enjoyed the support of some of Durham's monks) was formally installed.

The north transept (left), crossing tower and nave

Censure was provided by a papal document of 1372. This states that Durham's 56 resident monks (other members of the community were at daughter houses like Finchale Priory) enjoyed undertaking journeys in style, spending 'more on food and clothing' than befitted 'the modesty of their religion.' Although some serious misdeeds occurred, in general it appears that the standard of religious life practised at Durham was high.

Durham Cathedral Priory ceased to exist on 31 December 1539, during the Dissolution of the Monasteries, and St Cuthbert's shrine was destroyed. On 12 May 1541, however, Durham was reconstituted as one of the cathedrals of Reformation England. The first dean, Hugh Whitehead, and the 12 prebendaries were all members of the dissolved monastic community.

Description

Visitors usually first enter the imposing aisled nave of the cathedral. Here, the eye is caught by, among other things, incised patterns that adorn the cylindrical arcade piers. Furthermore, much of the aesthetic impact is derived from the fact that the nave is rib-vaulted. In addition, pointed transverse arches rise from every second pair of arcade piers. In effect, therefore, every two bays form a major bay, an arrangement derived from Jumièges in Normandy.

The nave is adjoined by the Galilee Chapel, added to the west end of the church, likely in the 1170s. The chapel is Transitional in style and contains the tomb of Bishop Langley who died 1437. Another tomb reputedly contains the bones of Bede, a revered Northumbrian historian who died in 735. In addition, the east wall is adorned by important survivals of medieval painting.

Heading eastward down the nave, one can see mutilated monuments in two bays of the south aisle. They are those of members of the Neville family of Raby. One of the tombs is that of Ralph, the second Lord Neville (d.1367) and his wife, Alice. Ralph was the principal English commander at the Battle of Neville's Cross in 1346, when an invading Scottish army was routed near Durham. He was the first layman buried in the cathedral.

Over the crossing, rises an impressive late 15th century tower, that replaced a less lofty one damaged by lightning in 1459. The crossing is flanked by transepts—both are rib-vaulted and have an east aisle. The south transept contains Prior Castell's Clock, which dates from the early years of the 16th century and stands on marble shafts.

East of the crossing, lies the aisled choir, the oldest part of the cathedral. However, the easternmost bay is a rebuild of the mid 13th century. In addition, the choir vault also dates from the mid 13th century. The Norman vault it replaced was apparently the first high-rib vault ever built in Europe.

The choir has splendid stalls. These date from the mid 1660s and were commissioned by Bishop John Cosin, a prelate fond of providing churches with impressive furnishings. East of the stalls, and on the south side of the choir, is the tomb of Bishop Hatfield (d.1381). It is located beneath an imposing platform, upon which stands the episcopal throne, said to be the highest in Christendom.

At the east end of the choir, behind the high altar, is the Neville Screen of c.1380, which originally had 107 alabaster figures. The screen is of Caen stone, was made in London, and largely paid for by John Neville of Raby. Immediately behind it, lies the feretory where the grave of St Cuthbert is marked by a simple slab in the floor.

In the 13th century, the east end of the cathedral was transformed by constructing the Chapel of the Nine Altars, a task that began in 1242 and continued for some forty years, and entailed rebuilding the easternmost bay of the choir. The Nine Altars is a wonderful example of mature Early English architecture, and there is a profusion of Frosterley marble shafts and lancet windows. Far more impressive, is the massive and magnificent Joseph window in the north wall. It dates from the 1280s and is one of the finest 13th century windows in England.

Looking down the spectacular nave towards the choir

The west walk of the cloister

Doorways in the south wall of the nave open to the cloister, which is enclosed by the church and former monastic quarters, some of which are not open to the public. This is true, for example, of the chapter house (in the centre of the east range) completed in the mid 12th century by Bishop Geoffrey Rufus. At the south-east corner of the cloister, is a tunnel-vaulted passage that leads southward to the cathedral close. East of this passage, stands the deanery, formerly the prior's lodging, which incorporates some of the earliest surviving work at Durham, i.e., from the episcopate of Walcher (1071–80) or perhaps even earlier. West of the passage, lies the south range whose first floor was the monks' dining hall. Off the southwest end of the range, is the remarkable kitchen (now a giftshop) built between 1366–74 and designed by the celebrated architect John Lewyn.

The undercroft of the west range, houses the cathedral treasury and restaurant. The first floor is occupied by the dormitory. Built between 1398–1404 on the site of a previous dormitory, it has its original timber roof and contains, among other things, an important collection of Anglo-Saxon sculpture.

Durham Cathedral is a World Heritage Site.

EASBY ABBEY

Easby Abbey lies beside the River Swale about a mile (1.6km) downstream from Richmond, and was founded in the 1150s by Roald, Constable of Richmond Castle, to house 13 Premonstratensian canons. The first abbot and canons came from Newhouse in Lincolnshire.

The initial endowment included the parish church of St Agatha at Easby, a structure dating from pre-Conquest times. The canons may well have worshipped in St Agatha's for thirty years or so before starting to construct the monastic church in about 1180. Alternatively, they may have worshipped in a temporary wooden structure.

Easby suffered from Scottish raiding parties during the 14th century. Hence, in 1318, the tax assessment of the abbey and its estates was reduced from £162 to £40. Moreover in 1346 an English army, billeted at Easby en route to confront David II of Scotland, caused severe damage.

Easby had 19 canons and a lay brother in 1380–81. From 1333 patronage of the abbey was in the hands of the Scrope family of Bolton in Wensleydale, who

The imposing refectory from the southwest

Inside the refectory, facing the attractive east window

remained patrons until the Dissolution. Their connection with the house was prominently displayed through heraldry, a point noted in 1386 by the abbot who testified to its presence 'throughout the church of St Agatha in glass windows, and on panels before the altars, on vestments of the said abbey, and in glass windows in their refectory.'

In 1478 Richard Redman, the representative in England of the abbot of Prémontré, carried out an inspection of the monastery and concluded that the religious life practised was of a high standard. In contrast, in 1494 the house was censured for becoming lax.

Easby was closed by the Crown in 1536. Later that year, however, during the rebellion known as the Pilgrimage of Grace, canons were restored to the monastery by rebels. After the end of the revolt, Easby Abbey was permanently suppressed in 1537.

Description

The layout of the monastery was unconventional. For example, the dormitory lay in the west range of claustral buildings rather than in the east range. This was done so that the latrine block, adjoining the dormitory, could be flushed by water channelled from the Swale. Furthermore, the infirmary and abbot's quarters lay north of the church instead of to the east of the east cloister range.

Sadly, little of the church, located in the centre of the complex, survives. The church had an aisled nave, transepts (both with three eastern chapels), and a short square-ended chancel, lengthened by three bays in around 1340.

The cloister lies south of the nave. The claustral buildings, which have survived far better than the church, mostly date from the 13th century. As usual, the east range (which was enlarged in the 15th century by the construction of an upper storey of uncertain function) included the chapter house, whose windows were enriched with dogtooth.

The south range is dominated by the impressive remains of the refectory, a rebuild dating from about 1300 and erected over the vaulted undercroft of the previous dining hall. It is the most well preserved canons' refectory in the North, and the most eye-catching feature is the east window, which is dominated by a circle containing five trefoils. Hardly anything survives of the kitchen, located against the southwest end of the range.

The west claustral range, parts of which were two and three storeys high, included guest accommodation and the canons' dormitory. The westernmost part of the range comprised the latrine block: the canons had access to the top storey from their dormitory while, lower down, there was also access to the latrines from the guests' accommodation. Chris Given-Wilson has aptly observed that 'Although lacking in symmetry and beauty, the west range of Easby was an ingeniously planned and highly functional building.'

Easby Abbey is in the care of English Heritage.

EGGLESTONE ABBEY

Egglestone Abbey lies beside the River Tees a short distance downstream from Barnard Castle and was built to serve canons belonging to the Premonstratensian Order—the first members of the community came from Easby Abbey near Richmond in Yorkshire. They evidently did so in the 1190s and settled on land granted by a local landowner, apparently Ralph de Moulton.

In about 1205, the canons were joined by nine others when the abbey's limited resources were enhanced by a benefactor named Gilbert de Leya. Nonetheless, throughout its history Egglestone was not well endowed—the number of canons probably never exceeded 15—and the monastery often suffered from financial difficulties. At times, moreover, the community's income and solitude were rudely interrupted. In the early 14th century, for example, Scottish raiders penetrated deep into England and in 1323 the abbey was so severely plundered that the canons moved to other Premonstratensian houses until repairs were effected. Subsequently, in the 16th century, Egglestone was poorer than any other Premonstratensian house in England or Wales!

While some of the canons presumably lived devout lives, this was certainly not universally the case. An inspection carried out in 1502 revealed serious short-

The church with the nave on the left

One of the chancel's windows

comings. Hence the canons were ordered to cease quarrelling and to desist from going out of the abbey without permission. Boys were not to be allowed to sleep in the dormitory, and the abbot was to stop leasing estates for long periods without consulting the other canons.

Egglestone Abbey was closed during the Dissolution of the Monasteries. It was one of the last monasteries to go under—the end came on 5 January 1540.

Description

Substantial portions of the church and monastic buildings still stand. The church mostly dates from the second half of the 13th century when the original church was enlarged—the north wall of the nave, and most of its west wall, are however original. In contrast, the nave's south wall is late 13th century and has a fine series of contemporary windows between buttresses.

In the south transept, the outline of the original transept has been marked in the grass. Of its replacement, built c.1275, only the west wall remains. In the angle

The west wall of the south transept (left) and chancel

between the transept and the south wall of the nave, is a 15th century stair turret that rose to a crossing tower. Only low foundation walls survive of the north transept.

A large black tomb chest lies in the centre of the crossing. It contained the remains of Sir Ralph Bowes. In a will drawn up in the summer of 1482, Bowes—the lord of Streatlam near Barnard Castle—stated that he wished to be buried in the abbey.

The chancel dates from the first phase of the church's enlargement, which commenced around 1250. The east wall has a five-light window with mullions devoid of tracery—if not the result of subsequent restoration, the window was highly unusual for the period.

Untypically, the monastic buildings lay to the north of the church rather than on the south side. In line with common practice, though, they were ranged around a cloister that adjoined the church.

The west and north ranges have all but vanished—the upper floor of the latter served as the canons' dining hall. In contrast, the east range, which included the dormitory at first floor level, has survived to a much greater degree but is not entirely medieval. The range was substantially changed in the second half of the 16th century when it was converted into a private residence. At its north end lies the reredorter— the building that contained the monastic latrines. The drainage channel running along the north side is well preserved. It was flushed by water diverted from nearby Thorsgill Beck and the effluent was carried into the Tees.

Egglestone Abbey is cared for by English Heritage. There is no entrance fee.

FINCHALE PRIORY

L ocated beside the River Wear, a few miles downstream from Durham City, Finchale Priory is best known for its association with a saintly hermit named Godric. He was born near the Wash in about 1065, and became a merchant with trading links in countries as far apart as Denmark and the Holy Land, and possibly also dabbled in piracy.

In the early years of the 12th century, when living with an elderly hermit at Wolsingham in County Durham, Godric was reportedly told in a vision that St Cuthbert—the North's premier saint—would provide him with a place for a hermitage of his own at Finchale (pronounced 'Finkle'), a location unknown to him.

Later, in about 1112, after carrying out a pilgrimage to Jerusalem and spending time at Whitby, Godric moved to Finchale with the blessing of Ranulf Flambard, the Bishop of Durham, who granted him the site. Apparently, Godric first lived at a spot about one mile (1.6km) upstream, before moving to the present location after a couple of years or so where he built a small hut and an adjoining chapel. Following a flood in around 1149 that almost claimed his life, Godric, to offer thanks for his deliverance, constructed a more substantial place of worship, dedicated to John

The ruins of Finchale Priory overlook the River Wear in a wonderful setting

the Baptist. He linked the new building to his previous chapel by constructing a walkway with a thatched roof.

At some point, Godric accepted the supervision of Durham Cathedral Priory. From members of the Durham community, Godric received instruction. Monks also travelled to Finchale on a regular basis to say Mass. Furthermore, as Godric's health declined, a monk was sent to live with him. Godric died at Finchale on 21 May 1170 at the ripe old age of around 105.

For some years after this, Finchale was a hermitage used by Durham monks. However, in 1196 a baron named Henry du Puiset founded a monastery at Finchale as a daughter house of Durham.

By the time Finchale Priory was established, Godric's tomb had become a place of pilgrimage. Although he never received papal canonization, he was widely viewed as a saint in the region and people with ailments visited Finchale in the eager hope of receiving a miraculous cure at his tomb. According to R. Finucane, 70 per cent of those reportedly cured by Godric were female. As women were excluded from St Cuthbert's shrine at Durham, presumably the majority of those who sought a cure at Finchale were members of the fairer sex.

The size of the monastic community was always small and peaked at 15 in 1278. During the 14th century it was decided to make Finchale a retreat for monks from Durham Priory. Exactly when it became a 'holiday place' is uncertain, but a reference of 1346 shows that the practice was well established.

In 1408, it was decreed that monks from Durham would travel to Finchale in groups of four and spend three weeks in the company of the resident community, a prior and four monks, before another party would take their place. On alternate days, the visiting monks either had to keep the usual round of religious services or could walk 'religiously and honestly' in the fields except for attending Mass and Vespers: a routine they conducted in pairs. Finchale's role as a retreat for monks from Durham continued until it was closed in 1538 during the Dissolution of the Monasteries.

Description

The enchanting ruins lie in a loop of the River Wear and are overlooked by high ground clad in trees. This is especially true to the north, where steep limestone cliffs are crowned by ancient woodland.

The church, erected in the 13th century, has a typical east-west axis. Initially, the chancel was flanked for most of its length by aisles. In the mid 1360s, however, these were demolished—presumably to save the cost of repairs—and the arches that had opened into them were blocked and provided with windows. Interestingly, the chancel contains low remains of an earlier structure, Godric's chapel dedicated to John the Baptist, and the outline of the rest of this building is marked in the turf. Moreover, in the grass, a stone cross indicates the site where Godric was buried.

The crossing was the only part of the church with a stone ceiling and was

Looking down the church from the chancel

surmounted by a low tower with a spire. The tower was supported by four cylindrical columns. The largest contains a spiral stair that climbed to the tower.

Much of the fabric of the transepts still survives. This is also true of the nave. The latter originally had aisles but during the programme of alterations in the 1360s, the north aisle was demolished. At the same time, the south aisle was transformed into the north walk of an enlarged cloister adjoining the south side of the nave.

Around the cloister are the remains of various structures. These include the chapter house in the east range—a range whose upper floor contained the monks' dormitory. The chapter house still has its entrance arch with flanking windows, and around the walls of the room one can see the stone seats where the monks sat. On the south side of the cloister, are the substantial remains of a building that contained the monks' refectory. In contrast, little survives of the cloister's west range, which may never have been completed.

East of the cloister, lie the monks' latrine block, and the kitchen, where the remains of an oven are clearly visible. Further east are the ruins of the prior's fine home—which included a study and chapel—and from where the prior could enjoy views of the River Wear and the woodland beyond.

Finchale Priory is cared for by English Heritage.

FOUNTAINS ABBEY

The ruins of Fountains Abbey, one of the most famous monastic sites in Europe, stand in a lovely setting near Ripon in North Yorkshire.

Fountains was the second Cistercian monastery established in the north of England. It followed close on the heels of Rievaulx, for on 27 December 1132, Thurstan, the Archbishop of York, granted 13 monks land in the narrow valley of the River Skell upon which to found their own abbey. The monks had recently left the wealthy Benedictine monastery of St Mary in York, where they had clashed with the elderly abbot who resisted their calls for him to make life in the monastery more austere.

Reportedly, the site they received from Archbishop Thurstan was 'thickset with thorns, and fit to be rather the lair of wild beasts than the home of men.' We are told that this was so in an early 13th century account, partly based on the reminiscences of an elderly monk named Serlo, an early member of the Fountains' community. What is certain is that there was a good supply of water, for in addition to the Skell there were several springs (*fontes*) after which the abbey became known.

In 1133, the monks requested admission to the tough Cistercian Order. In response, Bernard of Clairvaux—the dominant figure in the Cistercian world—sent

A general view of Fountains Abbey

a monk named Geoffrey d'Ainai to Fountains in order to supervise the formation of a Cistercian monastery. Geoffrey 'had set in order and established many monasteries' and under his direction timber buildings, including a small church that replaced a wattle chapel, were constructed on a new site just to the west.

Initially, Fountains was poor and struggled to survive. Its prospects improved decisively in 1135 when three wealthy canons of York Minster joined the community. They brought with them their wealth and respectability, as well as a fine library. By October of that year, the number of monks had climbed to 35. Work on a simple modest stone church commenced in 1136. Meanwhile, the community's resources were being enhanced by grants of land from wealthy laymen.

In 1144 a formidable Yorkshireman named Henry Murdac (a former monk at Clairvaux) became abbot and promptly supervised a major and rapid construction programme. This included building substantial quarters ranged around a large cloister, a development that entailed redirecting the Skell approximately 84ft (26m) to the south.

During Murdac's abbacy, Fountains was engaged in a bitter dispute with the Archbishop of York, William fitzHerbert. In 1146 matters became so heated that supporters of the primate descended on Fountains and sacked the abbey and set fire to its buildings. 'They had no respect for the order,' states the source mentioned above, 'they had no respect for the altar. The holy brotherhood stood by and saw with sorrow in their heart' the devastation wrought.

In 1147, the unsatisfactory archbishop was removed from office and replaced by Murdac, who nevertheless maintained a keen interest in Fountains, where restoration work commenced. Furthermore, in 1146–7 three bands of monks from the abbey left to found daughter houses (others had already done so in the late 1130s) and their departure may have been due to a need to reduce the size of the abbey's community while repairs were carried out.

In the 1150s Abbot Richard of Clairvaux (1150–70), began replacing the restored church with a much more impressive structure that was completed under his rule. Moreover, in the late 1150s, work started on enlarging (and partly rebuilding) the claustral quarters in order to meet the needs of an expanding community. This construction programme lasted for approximately 30 years and was on a grander scale than at any other Cistercian house in the country.

Further significant building took place in the first half of the 13th century. For example, Abbot John of Kent (1220–47) enlarged the church by erecting the transeptal Chapel of the Nine Altars. By this date, Fountains was at the height of its prestige and was the country's wealthiest Cistercian house.

Much of its income was derived from heavy involvement in the wool-trade, and the monastery's fortunes took a sharp turn for the worse in the second half of the century partly as a result of poor management. The abbey gambled heavily on the wool-trade by entering into contracts years in advance of a wool clip. When the clip fell below that of the contract, the monks were compelled to make up the deficit by buying in wool to supply the merchants. This led to major financial problems. By 1291 debts totalled the vast sum of £6,373.

In the early 14th century, the situation was exacerbated by Anglo-Scottish warfare. Scottish incursions dramatically reduced the abbey's income from a number of its estates. In 1318, the Scots made their presence felt directly when they briefly occupied the monastery.

Although it was still an important house, the abbey's fortunes remained at a low ebb until the mid 15th century. In 1380–81, for instance, the community only comprised 34 monks and 10 lay brothers, well below the days when numbers may have been as high as 120 monks and 400 lay brothers.

In November 1539 Fountains Abbey, the wealthiest Cistercian house in Britain, was surrendered to the king by the last abbot, Marmaduke Bradley. At the time of its surrender there were 32 monks.

Description

The austere aisled nave of the church dates from the 1160s and is entered via an elaborately moulded doorway. However, the dominant feature of the west front is a massive window inserted by Abbot Darnton in 1494 and now sadly devoid of tracery.

The nave has an arcade and clerestory, for like many other Cistercian churches there is no middle storey, and the arcade arches are carried by sturdy cylindrical piers. Although vaults covered the aisles, the main span of the nave had a wooden roof, boarded in to give the impression of a vault, and this was also true of the transepts.

The crossing tower no longer survives, and only the northwest and southeast piers that supported it remain to their full height. The south transept is essentially as built in the 1150s and is even more austere than the nave. The elevation is again of two stages. Three tall pointed arches, on the east side of the transept, each opened into a chapel and only the south chapel has remained as first built. Originally, the north transept was identical but major changes were made by Abbot Huby in the early 16th century. For one thing, the arches of the central and northern chapels were blocked in order to strengthen the east wall of the transept—the south chapel had been demolished in the early 13th century. The changes were necessitated by the construction of Huby's Tower against the north side of the transept. The impressive tower rises 160ft (48.8m) and is crowned by an embattled parapet.

In the early 13th century the chancel was demolished and replaced by a vaulted one in the fashionable Gothic style. Much of the main body of the new chancel, which had a two storey elevation, has not survived. On the other hand, the aisle walls stand almost to their full height. In each bay, above trefoil-headed arcading, is a lancet window flanked by lower blank lancets.

The Chapel of the Nine Altars adjoins the east end of the chancel, and has survived virtually intact, albeit devoid of its roof and vaults. The elevation is again of two storeys and, as in the chancel, there is trefoil-headed blind arcading. The

The nave, Huby's Tower and west range

Looking down the church from the nave

chapel had an attractive multi-coloured tiled floor and was primarily lit by two tiers of tall lancets. In 1483, Abbot Darnton inserted a massive window in the east gable.

The cloister, adjoining the south side of the nave, is about 125ft (38m) square. The principal room at ground floor level in the east range is the chapter house, one of the largest in England. It dates from the 1160s. Two rows of columns of grey Nidderdale marble divided the room into three aisles and partly supported a vault. Tiers of stone benching against the walls served as seating for the monks. Several abbots were buried in the chapter house, and one of the graves is that of John of Kent. At first floor level, the monks' dormitory ran the length of the east range and, following its extension in the 1160s, could accommodate around 120 monks.

The south cloister range dates from the abbacy of William of Newminster (1180–90) and the main room was the monks' refectory. A tasteful example of the Early English style, the dining hall projects southward, well beyond the rest of the range and the far end is held above the River Skell by a vaulted tunnel. The refectory, primarily lit by shafted lancets, was divided in two by a central arcade of pointed arches carried on piers and corbels of Nidderdale marble.

The west range is the longest. It measures 300ft (91.5m) by 42ft (13m), and the

Rib-vaulting in the west range

southern four bays are carried across the Skell by four tunnels. It was mostly built between the late 1150s and the 1170s. The rib-vaulted ground floor contained the lay brothers' refectory, and was also used for other purposes such as storage. The entire upper floor comprised the lay brothers' dormitory and could easily accommodate up to 400 men.

Other structures at Fountains include the remains of high status guestshouses. There are also two latrine blocks, linked to the east and west ranges, which, respectively, served the monks and lay brothers. Moreover, extensive vestiges of the monks' infirmary lie east of the claustral ranges, and mostly date from the abbacy of John of Kent. His construction of the Chapel of the Nine Altars entailed the destruction of the earlier infirmary. Owing to limited space for the new infirmary buildings, a remarkable feat of engineering was undertaken. Four great parallel tunnels were constructed to channel the Skell and provide a platform upon which the infirmary could be erected.

The extensive and impressive ruins at Fountains lie in enchanting surroundings and are justly famous. Indeed, Fountains Abbey is a World Heritage Site. It is managed by the National Trust but the preservation of the buildings is undertaken by English Heritage.

A tranquil scene – the abbey from the east

GREYFRIARS, RICHMOND

I n 1258 a Yorkshire baron named Ralph fitzRandal, the lord of Middleham in Wensleydale, founded a house for Franciscan friars on the northern outskirts of Richmond.

The Franciscan Order, whose members were also known as Grey Friars, arrived in England in 1224 and was committed to the ideal of preaching. Hence the site of the friary at Richmond, near a centre of population, was ideal.

When the Grey Friars settled at Richmond, Anglo-Scottish relations were peaceful but in the 1290s warfare commenced and the violence that ensued, which included cross-border raids by the enemy, affected Richmond. In 1313, the borough thus commenced erecting a town wall. This was provided with a postern gate (still extant) that gave access from the town to the friary. In 1315, moreover, the Archbishop of York instructed the head of Richmond's Franciscan community to preach against the Scots and to urge the populace to resist the enemy.

Benefactors of the friary included John of Brittany, the Earl of Richmond, who bequeathed £5 to the friars in 1304, and Sir Richard le Scrope and William de Huddeswell who, in 1364, granted the friars four acres for the 'enlargement of their property.' In addition, Scrope (who was subsequently elevated to the peerage and built Bolton Castle in Wensleydale) left the friars £10 in his will of 1400.

In the meantime, during a lawsuit waged in 1386–87, it was recorded that the friary buildings included a guesthouse, built about 50 years earlier, and a washroom 'where the friars commonly wash themselves when they come to the house tired and weary'.

During the course of the friary's existence changes were made to the church. A south aisle was added during the 14th century, and in the 15th century an imposing tower was erected between the nave and the chancel and presumably replaced a less grand tower.

In the second quarter of the 16th century, John Leland wrote as follows: 'Grey Freres [lies] a litle withowt the waullis. Their howse, medow, orchard, and a litle wood, is waullid yn. Men go from the market place to hit by a posterne gate.' Leland also noted that the friary was the only place at Richmond that had a conduit to supply water.

The friary was closed down in 1539, at which time the community comprised a warden and 13 friars.

Description

The remains of Greyfriars stand in the pleasant grounds of the Friary Memorial Garden, located beside the main road that runs through Richmond. Not much has survived above ground. The claustral buildings no longer exist, and most of the church has likewise vanished. Indeed, the only substantial survival is the imposing 15th century tower that stood between the nave and the chancel. It is the most northerly monument of the order standing in England, an impressive, eye-catching feature, that has been described by Henry Thorold as 'every inch a Franciscan tower.'

The eye-catching tower

GUISBOROUGH PRIORY

The Augustinian priory at Guisborough was probably founded in or around the year 1119 by Robert de Brus of Skelton, the most powerful man in northeast Yorkshire and a close companion of Henry I.

Brus gave the priory a rich endowment, mostly of moorland, which was subsequently enhanced by grants from other members of his line and other leading Yorkshire families. Indeed, according to Janet Burton, by 1135 'the canons of Guisborough were in control of wide tracts of land, the service of tenants, and eleven churches, and for the purposes of building they enjoyed free access to materials from Eskdale forest.'

Furthermore, in 1263 Henry III granted the canons the privilege of holding a weekly market and an annual three-day fair in the neighbouring town of Guisborough, which had been granted to them by Robert de Brus. Thus the king substantially added to the income of the monastery.

Although wealthy, Guisborough Priory (sometimes also spelt 'Gisborough') enjoyed a reputation for the sanctity of its religious life, at least during the 12th century. In 1280, though, the Archbishop of York conducted a visitation and found much amiss. For example, the infirmary was filled with canons feigning illness.

Robert de Brus was buried in the substantial priory church in 1151. This was also true of several of his descendants, one of whom was the grandfather of Scotland's king, the redoubtable Robert the Bruce (1306–29).

Presumably to serve the needs of an expanding community, in the closing decades of the 12th century it was decided to replace the priory church with a larger structure. Building work appears to have continued on the church into the mid 13th century, and thereafter on the claustral quarters.

On 16 May 1289, after soldering cracks in the lead over the south transept, a workman placed his iron pans with their burning coals on the beams. He then left his assistants to put them out, while he descended from the roof. However, they failed to do so properly, and the roof soon ignited and a devastating fire ensued.

Damage was such that work on a new church began in 1290. Nevertheless, archaeological excavation and an analysis of the fabric have shown that a significant amount of the damaged place of worship was retained and incorporated in the new structure. The building programme finished in the late 14th century. While work progressed, the easternmost five bays of the nave evidently functioned as a temporary church. Judging from what remains of the new church, it must have been, in essence, a masterpiece of the Decorated style.

The cost of rebuilding took its toll on the finances of the priory, as did Scottish raids that devastated its northern estates in the early decades of the 14th century. To make matters worse, Guisborough had to accommodate displaced canons from

The imposing east wall of the chancel

other affected houses such as Hexham and Brinkburn. Later, in 1375, permission was granted for its buildings to be fortified.

Guisborough's fortunes subsequently improved. Indeed, in 1535 its income was over £628. It was thus the fourth wealthiest house in Yorkshire and the county's richest Augustinian community. Guisborough was formally dissolved in April 1540 and was one of the last houses in England to be suppressed. At the end, the community comprised the prior and 24 canons.

Description

Sadly, most of the fabric has not survived. Remnants of the once imposing monastery include part of the late 12th century gatehouse. Its south wall has two arches, and the largest of these provided access for carts whereas its companion served pedestrian traffic.

Little remains of the church. Thankfully, however, the east wall of the chancel, supported externally by large square gabled buttresses, survives to its full height of 97ft (29.6m) and is a splendid fragment of Decorated architecture. It is dominated by a massive window whose great height has been enhanced by the fact that the wall beneath it was removed prior to 1709. This was done to form a vista in the formal gardens of a neighbouring post-Suppression house, Old Guisborough Hall, which was in turn demolished in the 19th century.

Of the claustral buildings, the east range, which contained the chapter house and dormitory, has not been excavated and this is also true of most of the south range, which housed the refectory.

Architectural detail of the east wall

In contrast, low walls belonging to the west range, which immediately post-dated the fire of 1289, are on display. The ground floor mostly comprised a vaulted under-croft used for storage. The upper floor contained the prior's lodging of a hall, chamber and chapel. The southern end of the west range was overlapped by the west end of the south range. At this part of the site, lies a vaulted service passage—running parallel to the south range—which was associated with the refectory and was adjoined by the kitchen.

Guisborough Priory is cared for by English Heritage.

The service passage

HEXHAM ABBEY

Hexham Abbey, or priory as it should correctly be termed, was probably founded by Thurstan soon after he became Archbishop of York in 1114 and was a house for canons belonging to the Augustinian Order. It lay in Hexhamshire, an outlying part of the archdiocese of York.

Centuries earlier, another monastery had existed at Hexham. It was established in the early 670s by Wilfrid, a leading Anglo-Saxon ecclesiastic. His church, whose underground crypt still survives, was built by craftsmen brought from Rome and lay where the church of the subsequent Augustinian priory was erected.

By 1138, the Augustinian priory had been provided with a cloister and stone monastic buildings erected immediately to the south of the old Saxon place of worship. The replacement of Wilfrid's church with a larger, Romanesque structure, followed and may indeed have already commenced. It is possible that the church—which would also serve as a place of worship for laity—had not been finished when, in around 1180, the decision was taken to start again and erect a new building on a far grander scale and in a different style. This construction programme continued into the 13th century and resulted in an imposing Gothic church.

Hexham Abbey from the south

On 28 June 1296, Scottish raiders set the monastery on fire, thereby destroying shrines, books and relics of saints. The following year, when most of the canons were resident elsewhere as a result, the Scots returned under William Wallace. He granted the canons a letter of protection on 7 November, possibly after they had agreed to pay protection money. Shortly thereafter, Wallace returned to Hexham again, and some of his men stole the chalice and other sacred altar vessels, action that annoyed and embarrassed their leader. On this occasion, Wallace remained at Hexham Priory for two days while his soldiers raided the neighbouring countryside.

Henceforth, until some point between 1320 and 1336, the priory was often deserted owing to destruction caused during Scottish raids, or through fear that history would repeat itself. Other Augustinian houses, in Yorkshire and Nottinghamshire, took in the displaced canons.

On 28 September 1536, royal commissioners arrived at Hexham intent on closing the priory on behalf of Henry VIII. They encountered opposition from the canons and townsfolk. One of the former, on top of the priory gateway, is described as confronting them 'in complete harness, with a strung bow in his hands'. In such circumstances, the commissioners withdrew. The priory thus had a temporary reprieve. In March 1537, though, the monastery was finally dissolved. However, the church survived and continued to serve as the parish church.

Description

Hexham Abbey lies at the heart of Hexham and dominates the market place. The church is, essentially, a fine example of the Early English style. Visitors first enter the south transept, which is covered by a timber ceiling but also has a rib-vaulted east aisle. The transept's most notable feature, and an exceptionally rare survival, is a straight flight of well-worn steps that gave the canons access to the church at night from their dormitory located to the south. At the foot of the night stair, is the late 1st century tombstone of a Roman soldier who belonged to a cavalry regiment evidently based at nearby Corbridge.

The crossing is surmounted by a low tower, and between the east pair of piers that partly support the tower, is a wooden rood screen erected in the early years of the 16th century by Prior Thomas Smythson. The screen separated the canons from lay worshippers and is adorned with paintings that include images of saints and bishops.

The nave is in the Decorated style. Although some of the fabric is medieval, almost the entire nave only dates from the years 1905–08 and doubt exists as to whether the nave was ever completed in the Middle Ages. The crypt of Wilfrid's church contained sacred relics and is located beneath part of the nave, from where stairs descend to the simple but fascinating survival from Anglo-Saxon times. The crypt is built of Roman stones, evidently brought from Corbridge. The main chamber is covered by a tunnel vault, which has much of its original plaster.

The north transept has a rib-vaulted east aisle and is rather more elaborate than

Looking towards the ornate north transept

the south transept, and evidently dates from a slightly later phase of construction. It has three very tall lancet windows in the north wall, and attractive blank arcading runs along the lowest level of this and the other walls.

The chancel has rib-vaulted aisles and mostly dates from the programme of rebuilding that began in around 1180. In contrast, the easternmost bay and east wall, the latter with two tiers of lancet windows, were rebuilt by John Dobson in 1858—the stained glass of the lancets was inserted in 1905.

At the west end of the chancel is a stone chair, carved from a single block, namely the Frith Stool or Wilfrid's Chair. This is a relic of Hexham's first monastery and is thought to date from around 675–700.

The stalls for the canons date from the 15th century and have misericords carved with various designs including shields, flowers and pagan 'Green Men' with leaf tendrils appearing from their nostrils.

The piers of the chancel arcades carry finely moulded arches. Some of the piers of the north arcade have capitals with stiff-leaf foliage, and are thus more ornate than the capitals of the south arcade.

The north aisle contains several Saxon grave covers. One can also see 15th century paintings on wooden panels depicting the Passion. Badly defaced monuments lie in the south aisle. One of these is of a cross-legged knight, namely Gilbert de Umfraville of Redesdale and Prudhoe, a senior Northumberland baron who died in 1307 after an interesting and sometimes villainous career.

The monastic quarters were ranged around a cloister on the south side of the nave. Little survives of the east range, which included the chapter house and, at first floor level, the canons' dormitory. Only fragments remain of the south range, which contained the refectory over an undercroft. On the other hand, much of the west range still stands, although not all the fabric is medieval. The most notable feature is the attractive lavatorium (against the exterior face of the east wall) which is believed to date from around 1300.

The lavatorium

HULNE PRIORY

Hulne, a former friary, lies in historic parkland on the western outskirts of Alnwick, and was evidently the first Carmelite house established in England. It was founded in 1242 by William de Vescy, the lord of Alnwick, for a group of hermits who had been forced to flee from Mount Carmel in the Holy Land, and preceded the Carmelites' second house in England, Aylesford in Kent, by several months.

Hulne lay within a hunting park of the lords of Alnwick and the community was granted permission to gather timber for building purposes from the park, as well as broom to serve as thatch, and honey and wax from wild bees in the woods.

Initially, the Carmelites—or White Friars as they later also became known—comprised groups of hermits. In 1247, however, following a meeting at Aylesford, they were formed into an order of friars and were modelled along Dominican lines. Although the Carmelites were the most contemplative friars, they were primarily an urban missionary order and, in marked contrast to Hulne, most of their nearly 40 houses in England were located in towns.

Hulne Priory was dissolved in 1539. At the time of its closure, it possessed a substantial library of 114 books that included histories, chronicles and works of philosophy. Anselm, Bede, and St Gregory numbered among the authors represented.

The secluded site of Hulne Priory

A general view, with the remnants of the church in the centre

Description

The ruins, which rank among the best preserved of any Carmelite foundation in England, stand on rising ground above the River Aln. They are enclosed by a curtain wall, erected in the 15th century, whose south side has a nondescript gatehouse near the centre.

A substantial amount of the south and west walls of the church still exist. Against the south side of the chancel, is a two-storey sacristy. The chapter house, in the east cloister range, projected eastward from the rest of the range, as did another building at the southeast end. The latter was probably the warming house, and was adjoined (to the east) by the friars' latrines. The south range contained the refectory, of which only the north wall survives. Little stands of the west range—a building at the north end is post-Dissolution and was a summerhouse erected in the 1770s. To the west of this structure, is a large rectangular tower built in 1486. Close to the gatehouse, is the 13th century infirmary, now a private residence. Finally, near to this, in the southwest corner of the site, are the fragmentary remains of domestic buildings.

Hulne Priory, which features as Maid Marion's residence in the 1991 film *Robin Hood: Prince of Thieves*, is open to visitors to Hulne Park (the property of the Duke of Northumberland) and there is no entrance fee.

JERVAULX ABBEY

T he story of Jervaulx Abbey, which lies beside the road from Masham to Middleham in North Yorkshire, begins in the days of King Stephen (1135–54). During that period, a baron named Acaris fitzBardolph gave a site near Fors in Wensleydale to a monk called Peter de Quincy and other monks of the Savigniac Order. According to a history probably written in the 1190s, Peter was 'very skilled and experienced in the art of medicine'. Evidently, he had served as a physician in the household of fitzBardolf's lord, Alan, Earl of Richmond and Count of Brittany. The earl also granted Peter and his two companions land and encouraged his knights to do likewise.

In 1149, shortly after the Savigniac Order had merged with the Cistercians, Fors became a dependent house of Byland Abbey, and early the following year Peter and his companions were joined by nine monks from that monastery. Conditions at Fors were very inhospitable, however. Therefore, in 1156 a more suitable location was provided. Conan, the new Earl of Richmond, granted the monks Jervaulx, a site approximately 16 miles (25.8km) further down Wensleydale and located on the south bank of the River Ure.

Looking across the cloister from the church towards the monks' dormitory

Jervaulx became a foundation of some wealth and importance (at the height of its prosperity it owned much of the dale) and gained a reputation for raising horses and producing cheeses and fleeces.

The last abbot was Adam Sedbergh. After the rebellion known as the Pilgrimage of Grace in 1536, a protest against Henry VIII's programme of closing monastic houses, the abbot was charged with involvement in the rising and confined in the Tower of London. Although Sedbergh had in fact done his best to avoid the rebels, he was executed.

As a result of the 'treason' of its abbot, Jervaulx was ruthlessly suppressed in the summer of 1537 and the monks were ejected without pensions. In that year, Sir Arthur Darcy, one of the commissioners involved in the Dissolution of the Monasteries, reported to Thomas Cromwell that the abbey possessed 'oon off the ffayrest churches that I have seen'. Sadly, the buildings at Jervaulx were either dismantled or blown up.

Description

There is little clinical about the site—the ruins are in private hands—and the place is enchanting, partly owing to the presence of a wide variety of flowers and weeping willows.

Only vestiges of the church remain. The most well preserved survival is the southwest doorway into the nave. Formerly used by lay brothers, the entrance dates from the late 12th century and has dogtooth ornament.

Parts of the fabric of the church date from the 1150s, as is true, for example, of some of the south transept, and were incorporated in a more substantial church—unusually, constructed from west to east—erected between around 1180 and the close of the century.

The east cloister range was constructed in the 1160s, but altered and extended later in the century. At the north end, a passage served as the library. The next part of the range was the chapter house, six steps below the level of the cloister. The room had a doorway flanked by round-headed windows that are still intact, and octagonal marble columns supported a rib-vault. Beyond this, lay a parlour as well as the day stair leading to the monks' dormitory (which occupied the whole of the upper floor of the range) and an undercroft believed to have originally accommodated novices. The west wall of the undercroft, and part of the dormitory, survive and form the principal feature of the site.

East and southeast of the dormitory are the remains of several buildings, including the monks' latrine block, the monks' infirmary, the abbot's quarters, and the substantial remains of a large meat kitchen erected in the late 15th century—fireplaces and ovens are visible in the north, west and south walls.

Next to nothing is visible of the south cloister range, rebuilt in around the 1180s, and whose main room was the refectory, a structure that projected southward from the rest of the range.

More substantial traces of the west range survive. It was the first part of the

The monks' infirmary from the south

abbey to be built and dates from the late 1150s. The range was the longest and contained the lay brothers' dining hall and dormitory. Projecting westward, from near the southern end, was their latrine block.

Jervaulx Abbey is open to the public and there is an honesty box.

KIRKHAM PRIORY

S tanding in lovely countryside beside the River Derwent in North Yorkshire, Kirkham Priory was founded in around 1121 as a house for Augustinian canons by Walter Espec, lord of Helmsley. At Kirkham, the parish church was part of the endowment, which included property elsewhere in Yorkshire and Northumberland, and formed the nucleus of the new monastery.

Legend maintains that Espec founded the priory in memory of his only son, who died in his presence in the vicinity following a riding accident. In fact, no record exists that he ever had offspring.

Within twenty years of its foundation, Kirkham almost became a Cistercian community. In the 1130s, apparently at Espec's bidding, a charter was drawn up to the effect that some of the canons would switch their allegiance to Cîteaux and stay at Kirkham. On the other hand, fellow canons who wanted to remain Augustinian, would leave to found a new monastery at Linton. The departing canons were to carry with them all their moveable goods, namely 'crosses and chalices, books and vestments, and everything belonging to the furnishings of the church.' They would

Kirkham's wonderful gatehouse

also take the stained glass windows and, to conform to Cistercian taste, these would be replaced with ones of clear glass. The plan, however, did not come into effect—perhaps most of the canons objected—and Kirkham stayed Augustinian.

In the 13th and 14th centuries, several heads of the de Ros family, lords of Helmsley (descendants of one of Espec's sisters) were buried in the priory church. Under the patronage of the de Ros line, an ambitious rebuilding programme commenced at Kirkham, where the church had already been largely rebuilt in the second half of the 12th century, but this proved a drain on the priory's resources and was not completed. Consequently, by the close of the 13th century the priory was heavily in debt and its finances remained at a low ebb during the 14th century. In 1321 debts exceeded £1,000. Matters were exacerbated by the Scots, and in 1328, Kirkham was one of several religious houses in Yorkshire that petitioned the Crown over destruction wrought on its property by the enemy.

Kirkham Priory was dissolved in December 1539, at which time there were 16 canons and two novices.

Description

The gatehouse, which gives access to the site from the north, is a wonderful piece of architecture and was erected in the late 13th century. It is adorned by, among other things, heraldic shields and pairs of carved figures depicting St George and the Dragon, and David and Goliath. Other statuary—flanked by windows with geometrical tracery—represents St Bartholomew, St Philip, and Christ.

Most of the church no longer survives. The low remnants of the aisleless nave contain fabric from two stages of construction in the 12th century. The north transept was entirely rebuilt during the programme of rebuilding in the second half of the 12th century, and the south transept was substantially altered at the same time.

In the 13th century, an impressive aisled chancel replaced a less grand aisleless predecessor, and as Glyn Coppack comments: 'From the surviving fragment of its east wall, eighteenth-century drawings and surviving fragments of loose architectural detail, it appears that the new church [never completed] was going to be one of the finest ever built in the north of England.'

On the east side of the cloister, lie the scant remains of the chapter house, a structure erected in the 13th century. From the south side of the chapter house, a late 13th century range runs off at a slight angle. This contained the dormitory which was not linked to the south transept, an unusual arrangement. Owing to the lie of the land, the northern part of the dormitory was at ground level whereas the southern half was supported by an undercroft.

The south end of the dormitory is adjoined, on a different alignment, by the canons' latrine block that survives almost to full height. The latrines were on the first floor, over a drain flushed with running water channelled down the hillside to the east. The drain ran westward towards the Derwent.

Stretching in a crescent shape north-eastward from the latrine block, were various

A fragment of the chancel's east wall

structures. These included the infirmary and the prior's quarters, built, respectively, in the late 13th century and early 14th century.

The south range of the cloister comprised a dining hall above an undercroft. Although the refectory was of late 13th century date, the doorway that opened to it from the cloister is 12th century and originally was perhaps located elsewhere on the site.

Near the doorway is a splendid late 13th century lavatorium (built into the southern end of the west wall of the cloister) ornamented by blank arcading and spheres containing cinquefoils and quatrefoils. Except for the wall containing the lavatorium, nothing remains of the west range. Indeed, one may never have been constructed.

Kirkham Priory is cared for by English Heritage.

LINDISFARNE PRIORY

The ruins of Lindisfarne Priory lie on Holy Island just off the coast of Northumberland. The monastery was founded on the tidal island in Norman times by Benedictine monks from Durham Cathedral Priory at a site previously occupied by a famous Anglo-Saxon predecessor, founded in 635 and celebrated for its association with pious churchmen such as Aidan and St Cuthbert.

The Saxon monastery was sacked by the Vikings in 793, and almost a century later the monks abandoned the vulnerable site after another Viking assault. The monks never returned and several generations passed before Lindisfarne Priory was established as a dependent house of Durham, likely in, or shortly before, 1122.

The priory was staffed by monks from Durham (which housed St Cuthbert's shrine) who usually did not stay long: they were either recalled or sent to one of Durham's other cells. Apparently, the number of monks present was so small that it was not until the late 12th century that there were enough for regular conventual buildings to be erected. Nevertheless, double figures were seldom if ever reached. By the early 15th century, in fact, the community had dropped to only three monks.

The priory's income, largely derived from property on the adjacent mainland, was badly hit by Anglo-Scottish conflict. In 1327 a monastic accountant bemoaned

The priory church, with the west front in the foreground

70

the fact that corn tithes annually worth over £100 before the commencement of hostilities in 1296, had dropped to £21 for that year.

During the 14th century, Holy Island frequently served as a harbour for royal purveyors of goods in transit to English armies campaigning in Scotland. Anxiety that this could lead to Scottish retaliation was possibly a factor that contributed to the monks' decision to fortify their priory. Among other things, a new perimeter wall with a wall-walk was constructed. Moreover the church was provided with low-pitched roofs with battlemented parapets, and arrow slits in the upper part of the west gable and perhaps elsewhere.

Lindisfarne Priory was dissolved in 1537, during the Dissolution of the Monasteries.

Description

Much of the church still stands to a good height and from the surviving remains, and old drawings, it is clear that although of modest size, the building was an elaborate structure. In fact, there is reason to believe that it was designed and built to echo Durham Cathedral. For instance, the cylindrical piers in the aisled nave were incised with chevron, diaper and fluting ornament. In addition, the entire church was vaulted. At this date in England it was uncommon for vaults to be provided throughout monastic churches, and Durham Cathedral is one of the few other examples.

At the crossing, a rib (popularly known as the 'rainbow arch') extends diagonally from the northwest to the southeast crossing pier and has aptly been described by Chris Given-Wilson as 'a fortunate survival, adding another dimension to our view of the ruin.' It has elaborate chevron moulding and is certainly a striking feature. In contrast, the crossing tower fell down in the late 18th century.

The transepts are small and have a shallow semicircular apse on their east side: each apse would have housed an altar. The aisleless chancel was originally also small and terminated with an apse. However, it was soon lengthened and provided with a straight end. The three large windows of the extension date from the 14th century and now lack tracery.

The monastic buildings are of grey stone—the masonry of the church has a red hue. Little remains of the east range, the last of the cloister ranges to be constructed, and here the chapter house had its longer axis parallel to the east cloister walk instead of at right angles to it, an unusual feature. The monks' dormitory lay above. Further to the south, stand the remains of a two-storey building whose ground floor served as the warming house, whereas the prior's main chamber was on the floor above. A large chimneystack that served both floors still stands and was built during a programme of reconstruction in the 14th century.

Scant remnants of the south range, which contained the monks' refectory, exist. In contrast, much of the west range (whose first floor may initially have served as the prior's lodging) can be seen and includes fabric that likely dates from the 12th century. Changes and additions were made in the 14th century. For example, a

View down the church from the nave

block containing a bakehouse and a brewhouse was built against the west end of the southern part of the range.

South of the claustral ranges lies the outer court, which housed ancillary structures that included accommodation for livestock. The court's perimeter wall stands to a good height and the remains of a gatehouse, that controlled entry into the court from the outer world, are located near the northwest corner of the perimeter.

Lindisfarne Priory is in the hands of English Heritage.

MOUNT GRACE PRIORY

T he ruins of Mount Grace Priory lie in a secluded location beneath the western escarpment of the North Yorkshire Moors and comprise the most well preserved Carthusian monastic site in England.

The monastery was founded in 1398 by Thomas Holland, the nephew and favourite of Richard II, who had made him Duke of Surrey the previous year. However, shortly after founding the priory, the duke's fortunes took a dramatic turn for the worse when Richard was overthrown, for in early 1400 Holland met his death while attempting to restore the deposed king.

For a number of years following Holland's execution, Mount Grace (the last monastery founded in Yorkshire before the Reformation) was in a precarious financial position. In 1415, for example, Henry V took some of the priory's lands over in order to grant them to a Carthusian monastery that he was founding in the south of England.

Carthusian monks led far less communal lives than members of other religious orders and so the monks at Mount Grace spent most of their time alone in individual

The church from the southwest

Looking towards one of the springs that supplied water

cells ranged around a vast cloister whose longest side measures 272ft (83m).

The first cells were of timber, but from the 1420s onward they were rebuilt in stone. Next to the entrance, each cell had a hatch in which food could be left for the monk to consume when required. The ground floor comprised a lobby, living room with fireplace, study, bedroom and oratory. The floor above this served as a work-shop. At the rear, the cell had a doorway opening to a garden which had a lavatory located at the far end. In addition, the cells were provided with piped water, chan-nelled below ground from natural springs on the hillside overlook-ing the monastery. Water from other springs was channelled into drains to flush the latrines.

Unlike some other monastic orders, the Carthusians held learn-ing in high regard and Mount Grace itself produced scholars of merit such as Nicholas Love. In around 1410, when prior, he produced *The Mirrour of the Blessed Lyf of Jesu Christ* (which was in part a trans-lation of the *Meditationes Vitae Christi*), and of this work H.S. Bennett has commented: 'An outstanding writer...Love, used his Latin originals so skilfully that he produced a translation...which gives us some of the most beautiful prose of the century.'

Mount Grace was surrendered into royal hands in December 1539 during the Dissolution of the Monasteries. The community at the time comprised the prior and 16 other monks, as well as three novices and six lay brothers.

Description

The monastic complex is entered via a manor house that occupies the site of the priory's 15th century guesthouse, much of whose fabric it incorporates.

Upon walking through the manor house, one enters the inner court. In addition to the guesthouse, the inner court was partly enclosed by ranges of buildings that included stables, granaries, and a kiln-house where grain was dried and barley malted.

On its north side, the inner court is partly enclosed by the ruins of the church.

The church viewed from the inner court

This is a small structure, in line with Carthusian practise, and was significantly altered in the 1420s. For example a small tower, with an embattled and pinnacled parapet, was added. The church was also extended eastward. Subsequent changes included the construction of burial chapels on the north and south sides of the nave in about the 1470s.

East of the church lie the remnants of the lesser cloister, associated with the accommodation of lay brothers, whereas to the north one finds the great cloister. Around the latter were the monks' cells, as well as other structures such as the chapter house (which had access to the chancel of the church) and the refectory where the monks dined in silence on Sundays and feast days. On the north side of the great cloister, a cell (see the photograph on page 8) has been reconstructed and furnished authentically.

Mount Grace Priory is now managed by English Heritage.

RIEVAULX ABBEY

The majestic ruins of Rievaulx Abbey are located near Helmsley in North Yorkshire and are justly famous. Rievaulx was a Cistercian monastery founded in 1132 by Walter Espec, lord of Helmsley. On 5 March of that year, with Espec looking on, 12 monks from Clairvaux led by Abbot William (an able and well-educated Yorkshireman) settled at the site. An early 13th century work, states that they were 'men of extraordinary holiness and perfect piety...most worthy of the name of monk.'

Another source, written in 1167 by a member of the monastic community named Walter Daniel, says that the monastery was established beside 'a powerful stream called the Rye in a broad valley....High hills surround the valley, encircling it like a crown. These are clothed by trees of various sorts and maintain in pleasant

The beautiful setting of the ruins at Rievaulx

retreats the privacy of the vale, providing for the monks a kind of second paradise of wooded delight.'

Presumably, when the monks arrived, temporary timber quarters had already been provided by an advance party of lay brothers. Under Abbot William, modest stone buildings, including a church, were evidently built and a Clairvaux monk called Geoffrey d'Ainai who was skilled in setting out new Cistercian monasteries, apparently played a key role in this process. Moreover, during William's abbacy (1132–45) the church was soon replaced by a larger place of worship.

Rievaulx was intended to be a mission centre from which other Cistercian houses would be established and this rapidly occurred. In 1136 the first two daughter houses were founded, one of which, Warden in Bedfordshire, was on land granted by Espec.

The most celebrated figure in Rievaulx's history is Ailred (alternatively spelt 'Aelred'), a learned Northumbrian who became a monk at Rievaulx in 1134 and was elected abbot when aged 37. During Ailred's abbacy (1147–67) Rievaulx expanded notably and acquired great fame and a reputation for sanctity second to none. The number of monks grew to 140 and there may have been as many as 500 or more lay brothers. Such growth was inevitably associated with considerable building activity (a significant amount of the monastery, including the church, was pulled down and rebuilt on a grander scale) and much of the surviving fabric dates from this period. Ailred died on 12 January 1167. He had suffered from a malady that frequently plagued him during his last years, one so severe at times that he had lain on the ground in front of a fire 'twisted in pain like a sheet of parchment.'

The development of fine monastic quarters at Rievaulx was hindered by the River Rye, which ran down the centre of the valley and served as a boundary between it and a neighbouring monastery founded at Old Byland in 1143. Four years later, however, the community at Old Byland moved to a new site and therefore Rievaulx was able to divert the Rye, something it did on three occasions. Hence by the close of the century, the area available for the monastery's precinct more than doubled to approximately 100 acres (40.5 hectares).

Subsequently, various improvements and alterations were made to the church and other buildings. For example, in the 13th century the church was extended and enhanced by the construction of a splendid new chancel.

At times Rievaulx was heavily in debt, as was the case in the late 13th century. Its financial problems were mainly due to an epidemic of sheep-scab that devastated its flocks, which may have numbered approximately 14,000 sheep in 1275.

Rievaulx was also affected by the Scottish Wars of Independence. Indeed, in October 1322, a Scottish army defeated the English in a battle fought on high ground southwest of Rievaulx and proceeded to sack the monastery. Within decades of this event, the abbey was struck by the Black Death. By 1381–82 the community merely comprised the abbot, 14 monks and three lay brothers.

On 3 December 1538 Rievaulx was surrendered to royal commissioners, at which time there were 22 monks (including the abbot) and 102 servants. Its annual income at this date was £278. This indicates how far Rievaulx had fallen from its heyday for 28 other houses had incomes of £1,000 or more at this time.

Description

The late Sir Nikolaus Pevsner aptly commented: 'There is more left standing at Rievaulx than at any Cistercian abbey in England except Fountains; for the picturesque traveller it is an exquisite feast, and for the architectural historian what remains is of the highest interest.'

The splendid chancel

Little survives of the nave, apparently built in the 1150s. It was plain and severe. The elevation was of two storeys. A timber roof (likely of barrel-vaulted form) covered the main span of the nave whereas the aisles had stone barrel-vaults.

The transepts had timber ceilings and stand almost to their full height. The west walls are essentially 12th century, with dark brown masonry and tiers of round-headed windows. In the early 13th century, however, the transepts were largely rebuilt and heightened and the newer fabric is lighter in colour and superior in quality. The gable walls of the transepts are likewise both partly of 12th and 13th century date. In contrast, the east walls are entirely 13th century and have a three-storey elevation. A crossing tower constructed at this date has not survived.

Apparently, in the 1220s, work on an impressive vaulted three-storey chancel began. The chancel is one of the finest monastic buildings in the country, and the design includes clustered arcade piers that carry richly moulded arches, over which are the elegant triforium and clerestory.

The claustral buildings lie around a square cloister located south of the nave. The present east range dates from Ailred's time and includes a chapter house erected in the early 1150s. Its principal entrance is flanked by windows. In the mid 13th century, a shrine honouring the memory of the founding abbot, William, was inserted in the north window and remnants of this survive.

The main part of the very unusual chapter house comprised a two-storey rectangular room (probably covered by a timber barrel-vault) with an apsidal east end. The room was enclosed by an arcade and low rib-vaulted aisles: the latter were entered from the cloister via doorways either side of the principal entrance. The arcade, fronted by three tiers of stone seats, had cylindrical piers and supported a clerestory.

The upper floor of the east range was occupied by the monks' dormitory, which ran southward from the south wall of the chapter house—access to the church was via a passageway located over the vestibule of the chapter house. Originally the dormitory was 245ft (75m) long by 34ft (10.3m) and capable of housing the 140 monks recorded as present at Rievaulx in the 1160s. Later, in around 1400, the dormitory was truncated.

At ground-floor level, a passage led eastward through the range to another cloister—the infirmary cloister—and its associated buildings erected in the 1150s. The north side of the cloister was enclosed by a two-storey structure built to accommodate Ailred when, contrary to custom owing to his declining health, the General Chapter of the Cistercian Order decreed that he should dwell apart from the community. It is the earliest known example of such a building in the order, and was used as a residence by later abbots.

The east side of the infirmary cloister was bounded by the infirmary, whose remains constitute the earliest surviving Cistercian infirmary in Britain. The structure was spacious and well lit. Beds were located in an east aisle, partitioned to provide a degree of privacy. In the closing years of the 15th century, John Burton,

The chapter house (foreground) overlooked by the south transept

Rievaulx's extensive ruins—buildings associated with the infirmary cloister are in the foreground

the head of the community, transformed much of the building into one of the largest abbot's houses in England.

The south side of the infirmary cloister was enclosed by a three-storey building, erected on lower ground. The upper floor, here, contained the monks' latrines, accessible from their dormitory. A row of privies along the south wall discharged into the abbey's main sewer.

The south range of the main cloister was dominated by the very impressive monks' refectory, which projects southward from the rest of the range and was lit by many lancet windows. The refectory was built in the late 12th century (owing to the terracing of the site it was erected upon an undercroft) and replaced an earlier dining hall aligned parallel to the south walk of the cloister.

The west range was constructed in around 1140, but was subjected to remodelling on more than one occasion. It housed the lay brothers. In the monastery's heyday, some lay brothers may also have been accommodated in part of the east range.

Rievaulx Abbey is cared for by English Heritage.

St MARY'S ABBEY, YORK

The abbey of St Mary in York, one of the wealthiest and most important monasteries in medieval England, was founded in the late 11th century by William II.

Stephen, the first abbot, had previously led a religious life at Whitby and Lastingham. From the latter site, he and fellow monks made their way to the church of St Olave, just outside York. However, that location was not suitable for an abbey and when William II visited York in 1088 he granted Stephen and his colleagues the site upon which St Mary's was duly built.

Trouble erupted at St Mary's in late 1132. Earlier in the year, a party of Cistercian monks en route to found Rievaulx, stayed at the abbey before completing their journey. These austere figures evidently had a profound effect on 13 of the monks. So much so that they expressed disenchantment with the comfortable state of affairs in the monastery and wanted Geoffrey, the elderly abbot, to pursue a more demanding monastic life. However, he did not share their enthusiasm and bad blood developed.

News of the dispute reached Thurstan, the Archbishop of York. On 9 October he thus visited St Mary's to achieve a settlement. Tempers were running high and soon led to a brawl. Amid the uproar, Thurstan placed the abbey under an interdict and, after sheltering in the church with the discontented monks, left the premises with them. He soon granted the monks a site at Fountains upon which to found a monastery of their own.

In 1195 the Archbishop of Canterbury, Hubert Walter, visited St Mary's (which had been badly damaged by fire in 1137) and did so because the Archbishop of York was suspended at the time. Hubert heard complaints from the monks about their abbot, Robert of Harpham, and as a result the abbot was deposed.

Conflict sometimes erupted between the abbey and the mayor and citizens of York. This was certainly the case in the reign of Henry III. Indeed, in 1262, the matter was so serious that several of the abbot's men lost their lives and some of the abbey's property was damaged. Simon of Warwick (elected abbot four years earlier) fled and was absent for two years. He remained in office until his death in 1296 and oversaw a major construction programme that began in 1271 and witnessed the rebuilding of the church.

Archbishop William Melton of York held a visitation of St Mary's in March 1319, and duly observed that there were no serious offences in the standard of monastic life practised. He did, however, note that the abbey was in debt to the tune of over £4,000, a massive sum. The monks were thus instructed to avoid needless expense.

In 1535 one of Melton's successors, William Lee, ordered St Mary's to adhere strictly to the Benedictine Rule and declared that the abbot, William Thornton,

The attractive remnants of the abbey church

should stop associating with a married woman named Elizabeth Robinson and stay in the monastery unless he was engaged on legitimate business.

Thornton, who had been elected abbot in 1530, was still in office when St Mary's was closed in 1539 during the Dissolution of the Monasteries, at which time the abbey was worth over £2,000 a year.

Description

The ruins of St Mary's Abbey are located in the grounds of Yorkshire Museum Garden, west of York Minster. The fortified wall that enclosed the precinct still stands and the main gatehouse is in Marygate.

Sadly, most of the church has gone. What survives includes part of the west wall, ornamented with blank arcading, and the wall of the north aisle of the nave, an elegant composition with blank arcading and windows that have fragments of geometrical tracery. The most eye-catching part of the church is the imposing northwest crossing pier from which an arch extends to the aisle wall.

The cloister lay to the south of the church and some of the claustral buildings have been incorporated in later structures.

TYNEMOUTH PRIORY

Tynemouth Priory lay on a commanding headland just to the north of the mouth of the River Tyne and was enclosed by Tynemouth Castle. The monastery—located on the site of an Anglo-Saxon predecessor—was founded in about 1090 by Robert de Mowbray, the Earl of Northumberland, as a Benedictine house dependent on St Albans Abbey in Hertfordshire.

Monks from St Albans thus formed the nucleus of Mowbray's foundation, the first post-Conquest monastery in Northumberland. Mowbray generously endowed the fledgling monastic community, and throughout its history Tynemouth was St Albans' senior daughter house. Indeed, on the whole, it was one of the wealthiest Benedictine monasteries in the country.

In 1095, Mowbray rebelled against William II (the son and successor of William the Conqueror) and was captured at Tynemouth. At the time of his downfall, a major construction programme was underway on the headland. By 1110, work on the priory church was sufficiently advanced for the relics of a revered 7th century Northumbrian, St Oswin, to be placed in a shrine at its east end and Tynemouth became an important place of pilgrimage in the region.

Tynemouth Priory's dramatic setting

85

The church from the west

Around 1225, a monk who had come to Tynemouth from St Albans wrote a letter to a 'dear brother' at the latter monastery and lamented: 'Day and night the waves break and roar and undermine the cliff. Thick sea frets roll in wrapping everything in gloom. Dim eyes, hoarse voices, sore throats are the consequence. Spring and summer never come here.' He also bemoaned the shriek of seagulls, the cries of drowning sailors, and the prominence of fish in the diet. It was not all bad news, though, for he says that the monastic church was 'of wondrous beauty.'

Tynemouth Priory lay in a part of Northumberland known as Tynemouthshire. With the Crown's permission, this liberty—which comprised several blocks of territory in Northumberland—was administered by the Prior of Tynemouth who appointed the necessary personnel. The liberty was founded by Robert de Mowbray but subsequently acquired additional rights and property. Within the liberty, which was moribund by the close of the Middle Ages, the prior retained all profits of justice and enjoyed numerous other prerogatives such as treasure trove and control of mines.

In the early 1290s, Tynemouth tried to break away from St Albans. The attempt was led by the prior, Simon of Walden, and a monk named John of Throckley. But the case they brought in the king's court failed and in the spring of 1294 the Abbot of St Albans, John of Berkhamstead, reasserted the authority of the mother house in no uncertain terms. One night, with a small force raised by a Newcastle merchant, he entered the priory and promptly arrested Walden and Throckley who were thus shipped south in chains.

During the period of Anglo-Scottish warfare that began in 1296, the defences at Tynemouth were strengthened. Much of the cost was borne by the priory, which was responsible for maintenance of the castle and a garrison. Prior Richard de Tewing (1315–40), who 'well and nobly ruled [Tynemouth]...with a strong hand,' maintained a garrison numbering 80 men.

In 1389 Tynemouth was attacked by the Scots. After this, grants from Richard II and northern landowners were made towards the cost of overhauling the defences and the ensuing building programme included the construction of the present gatehouse.

Monastic life at Tynemouth ended in January 1539, (the community at the time numbered the prior and 15 monks) when the priory was surrendered to the king. Tynemouth had been by far the wealthiest religious house in Northumberland, with an annual income of about £750 on the eve of its dissolution.

Description

Visitors enter the site via the late 14th century gatehouse and soon reach the ruins of the church, which was built in the Romanesque style between c.1090 and c.1120, but experienced additions and alterations during the priory's existence. The most notable changes occurred in the period from around 1195 to 1220 when a new chancel was constructed and the nave was extended westward.

A substantial amount of the building still stands. In particular, the east end of the chancel presents a dramatic spectacle. Indeed, it rises 73ft (22m) and dominates the site. It is Early English in style, and large lancet windows form a key element of the design. During the days of the priory, a coal fire was maintained in an open brazier on the top of one of the two turrets flanking the church's east wall to serve as a navigational aid for sailors.

The easternmost part of the church is the Percy chantry, a small, low structure, added in the mid 15th century. The chantry bears the name of Northumberland's foremost family, the Percys, one of the greatest families in English history, and has a very intricate vault with intersecting ribs joined by 33 sculptured bosses.

Very little, other than low foundation walls, remains of the monastic buildings. As usual, they were built to the south of the church and were centred around a cloister that adjoined the nave. The east range included the chapter house and dormitory, whereas the south range housed the refectory, and the west range was no doubt partly used for storage. In contrast, barns and agricultural buildings were mostly located to the north of the church.

Tynemouth Priory is in the care of English Heritage.

WHITBY ABBEY

The majestic ruins of Whitby Abbey, a Benedictine house founded in Yorkshire during the Norman period, stand on a headland that projects into the North Sea and dominates the historic and picturesque little town of Whitby situated below.

The abbey occupied a site where an Anglo-Saxon religious community had existed several centuries earlier. In 657, a double monastery—one that housed men and women—had been founded on the headland under an abbess of royal birth called Hild. Apparently, over two hundred years later, in around 867, this monastery was destroyed by the Danes.

Religious life ceased and the site became ruinous. However, soon after the Norman Conquest, a knight named Reinfrid visited Whitby and was deeply moved by the scene of desolation he beheld. Hence several years later, in around 1077, having renounced military life, Reinfrid returned to Whitby and under the protection of a Yorkshire baron called William de Percy, proceeded to revive the site.

Owing to the nature of the evidence, the exact course of events is uncertain. Some historians are of the opinion that Reinfrid established a hermitage in the monastic ruins, where he was soon joined by like-minded individuals, and that, following the arrival of a man named Stephen in about 1078, the community became monastic. Other scholars believe that Reinfrid and his colleagues lived a monastic existence from the outset.

Evidently, discord ensued and in the 1080s the community split. Stephen and some of the monks left and eventually founded St Mary's Abbey at York. Their former colleagues, who had to abandon Whitby as a result of piratical raids, sheltered several miles to the south at Hackness where some accounts maintain that Reinfrid was killed in an accident. Other sources say that he accidentally lost his life at Whitby before the pirate raids commenced.

Apparently, at some date after 1086 one of the monks at Hackness, a character named Serlo (William de Percy's brother) led his remaining colleagues back to Whitby. In around 1109, he was succeeded by another Percy, a nephew called William, who became Abbot of Whitby. On this point, Janet Burton comments, '1109 appears to mark the effective beginning of the existence of Whitby as an independent Benedictine Abbey.'

By the late 12th century, the community reportedly numbered about 40 monks. In the first half of the next century, the monks began replacing their Romanesque church—probably begun in the late 11th century—with a grander structure. This process evidently commenced in the 1220s and by around the 1250s an impressive new chancel had been erected. Work on replacing the transepts, erecting a crossing tower, and rebuilding the nave ensued. The construction programme probably ended in the 1280s and, in the case of the nave, was not pursued to a finish. Presumably, work ceased owing to a shortage of money and most of the old nave was left standing. The monks were nevertheless determined to proceed with construction work—a process that occurred intermittently—and the nave was eventually completed, possibly as late as the 15th century.

Whitby Abbey suffered as a result of Scottish incursions, and in 1316 the monks lamented that their 'corn and victuals' had 'been destroyed as well by the frequent inroads of the Scots as by accidents so that the Abbot and Convent have had to seek sustenance elsewhere.'

Archbishop William Melton of York carried out an inspection in 1320 and his report states that the abbey was heavily in debt. It also decrees that hunting dogs were no longer to be kept in the abbey precinct. The monks were also forbidden to leave the monastery carrying bows and arrows. Evidently, they had been engaging in sporting activity in Whitby Forest, of which the abbot was lord.

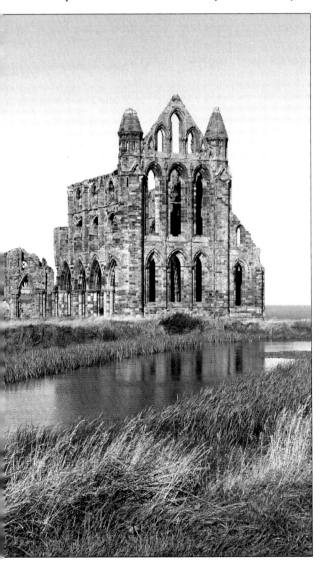

After the Black Death in the mid 14th century, the size of the monastic community declined. There were 22 monks when the house was surrendered to the Crown in December 1539.

Description

The ruins of the abbey mostly date from the 13th century and unfortunately, more than half of the church no longer stands—the south transept, for example, collapsed in 1763. Time has been even more unkind to the monastic buildings. They have vanished.

Of the nave, the most substantial remains are parts of the west end and the north aisle wall—some of what remains of the west front was rebuilt after being damaged by a German naval bombardment of Whitby in 1914.

Different phases of construction are readily apparent in the nave. For example, the westernmost of the windows in the north wall are large openings that

A dramatic spectacle—the east end
of the abbey church

Whitby's north transept (left) and chancel

were enriched by ornate tracery, and the style of the tracery indicates that they date from around the opening years of the 14th century. These windows are in marked contrast to slender lancets in the three east bays of the wall, which were erected in the 13th century.

The crossing tower collapsed in 1830, by which time of course the south transept (of which little survives) had likewise fallen. Fortunately, the north transept, whose vaulted east aisle was partitioned into chapels by wooden screens, still stands and is an imposing spectacle. For instance, the gable wall rises to full height and contains three tiers of lancets surmounted by a rose window.

Much of the 13th century chancel also exists. It replaced an apsidal Romanesque predecessor whose outline is marked in the turf. The fabric includes fine rib-vaulting along the north aisle (evidently the main span of the chancel was covered by a timber ceiling) and the east wall has three tiers of lancets, the uppermost of which are stepped. Of the chancel, John Goodall comments in the official guidebook: 'The choir of Whitby is remarkable for its extraordinary richness. Worked stone was extremely

A closer view of the chancel

expensive and here every surface dissolves into a profusion of carved detail and moulding.'

The main monastic buildings were ranged around a cloister located on the south side of the nave.

Whitby Abbey is in the care of English Heritage.

GLOSSARY

Aisle: passage alongside a nave, transept etc. of a church or the main body of some other building, separated from it by columns etc.

Apse: in churches, a semicircular or polygonal end to a chancel, aisle, etc.

Arcade: a series of arches supported by piers. *Blank* or *blind arcade*—series of arches supported by piers attached to the surface of a wall.

Barrel-vault: see 'Vault'.

Bays: divisions of a building defined by regular vertical features such as buttresses.

Boss: an enriched ornamental block usually covering the intersections of ribs in a vault.

Buttress: projecting mass of masonry or brickwork supporting a wall, or resisting the lateral thrust of a vault etc.

Capital: head of a column etc. It is normally decorated.

Chancel: the part of the east end of a church where the main altar is located. Also often applied to the entire east arm of a cruciform church—alternative expressions are choir and presbytery.

Chapter House: room where monks etc. met daily to hear a chapter of the monastic Rule and to discuss business.

Chevron: zigzag Norman ornament of the 12th century.

Choir: the part of a church where services are sung. Also often applied to the east limb of a cruciform church.

Claustral: pertaining to the cloister.

Clerestory: the upper stage of a church elevation and pierced by windows.

Cloister: in a monastic establishment, a covered walkway around an open quadrangle (garth).

Column: a vertical structural member typically consisting of a shaft with a base and a capital.

Corbel: a projecting stone or piece of timber to support a weight.

Crossing: the space at the junction of the nave, transepts and chancel.

Decorated: historical division of English Gothic architecture c.1290 to c.1340. A sumptuous style partly characterized by rich decoration of surfaces, flowing tracery, and lofty spires.

Dogtooth: typical Early English decoration consisting of a series of pyramidal flowers of four petals.

Early English: term applied to the style of English Gothic architecture of c.1190 to c.1290. An essentially refined style, chiefly characterized by lancet windows, which are often grouped together. Other motifs include columns surrounded by marble shafts, and dogtooth and stiff-leaf ornament.

Embattled: furnished with battlements.

Feretory: the place behind the high altar containing the principal shrine of a church.

Flying buttress: an arch or half-arch transmitting the thrust of a vault or roof from the upper part of a wall to a freestanding support.

Foil: Leaf-like ornamentation in windows etc. Trefoil, quatrefoil, cinquefoil—express the number of lobes in a shape.

Gable: area of wall (often triangular) at the end of a double-pitched roof.

Gallery: in a church, the intermediate storey above the aisle and below the clerestory, and looking through arches to the nave etc.

Gothic: a general term used for a style of architecture that appeared in England in the third quarter of the 12th century and lasted into the 16th century. Characteristic features include rib-vaults, pointed arches, flying buttresses, window tracery and spires.

Jamb: one of the straight sides of a doorway, window, etc.

Lancet window: slender window with a pointed arch.

Light: architectural term for a compartment of a window.

Moulding: a decorative band or edge.

Mullion: a vertical bar dividing a window into lights.

Nave: the western part of a church. In some monastic churches, it was where laity worshipped.

Norman: see 'Romanesque'.

Oratory: small chapel in a church or house for private devotions.

Order: one of a series of concentric stages—shafts for instance— receding towards the opening of a doorway etc.

Parapet: a low wall for protection at any sudden drop.

Perpendicular: the final phase of English Gothic architecture c.1340 to c.1530, and a marked contrast to the richness and great variety of the preceding Decorated phase. It is characterized by emphasis on straight verticals and horizontals. Among other characteristics are subdued window tracery and a fondness for lofty towers.

Pier: a strong vertical support for arches etc.

Pinnacle: a relatively small vertical structure capping a buttress etc.

Reredos: ornamental screen behind an altar.

Romanesque: a term applied to the style of architecture often called Norman in England, current in the 11th and 12th centuries. It is characterized by massively built walls, round arches, small windows, chevron ornament, very robust columns and clearly defined spatial units.

Rose window: circular window with patterned tracery around the centre.

Shaft: a slender column.

Stepped: progressively staggered.

Stiff-leaf: Early English foliage ornamentation consisting of many lobed shapes.

Tracery: ornamental work in the head of a window (and elsewhere such as on blank arcading) and usually formed by the curving and interlacing of bars of stone. Geometrical tracery, for example, was in vogue in the latter half of the 13th century and the early years of the 14th, and consists of circles or foils within circles.

Transepts: the transverse portions of a cross-shaped church.

Transitional: term applied to the architecture of c.1175-c.1190 during the transition from Romanesque to Early English.

Transverse arch: in vaulting, an arch that divides one compartment of vaulting from another.

Triforium: an arcaded gallery between the main arcade and the clerestory.

Turret: a small tower, usually attached to a building.

Undercroft: a vaulted room (sometimes below ground) beneath the principal upper room.

Vault: an arched stone ceiling, sometimes imitated in wood or plaster.
> *Barrel-* or *tunnel-vault*—one that looks like a continuous circular arch: the most basic vault.
> *Rib-vault*: a more attractive vault consisting of arched ribs and compartments of masonry between the ribs.

SELECT BIBLIOGRAPHY

Bond, J., *Monastic Landscapes*, 2004

Burton, J., *The Monastic Order in Yorkshire 1069-1215*, 1999

Butler, L., and Given-Wilson, C., *Medieval Monasteries of Great Britain*, 1979

Colvin, H.M., *The White Canons in England*, 1951

Coppack, G., *Abbeys and Priories*, 2006

Jennings, B., and Croucher, T., *The Yorkshire Monasteries: Cloister, Land and People*, 1999

Robinson, D., (ed.) *The Cistercian Abbeys of Britain: Far From the Concourse of Men*, 1998

Waites, B., *Monasteries and landscape of the North York Moors and Wolds*, 2007

ILLUSTRATION CREDITS

Hayley Austin: pp. 66, 68, 80, 90

Gavin Dodds: p. 6,

Glen Lyndon Dodds: pp. 8, 10, 11, 12, 14, 20, 21, 26, 27, 30, 31, 34, 35, 36, 38, 39, 40, 41, 53, 55, 56 (lower), 57, 60, 62, 63, 65, 73, 74, 75, 85, back cover

Shaun Dodds: title page, pp. 17, 18, 24, 28, 43, 56 (top), 59, 61, 70

Allan Harris: cover, pp. 51, 76, 78, 81

Angelo Hornak: p. 33

Gail Johnson: p. 72

Chris Maughan: p. 83

Pauline Mills: p. 89

Jonathan Oakley: pp. 44, 86

Ben Taylor: p. 91

OTHER ALBION PRESS TITLES

Running Shoes to Racing Silks is the fascinating auto-biography of Dave Dodds—a story that ranges from the North East of England to Southern Africa, and beyond.

The early chapters focus on the author's childhood and youth in Sunderland, where he was born just as the world was plunged into the Depression. In vivid detail, he recounts his days on Wearside during those grim years. Subsequent chapters recount the author's experiences in the merchant navy and as a factory worker, and chart his early exploits as an athlete on Wearside and elsewhere.

The scene then shifts dramatically, as Dodds embarked on a new life in Southern Africa, where he established himself as a leading long-distance runner before turning to another field of sporting endeavour, horseracing.

Themes also dealt with include the author's marriage, his far-flung holidays, and experiences during the war that ended white minority rule in Rhodesia, a conflict that brought his days in Africa to an end and led to his return to Sunderland.

The lively text, accompanied by a large selection of colour and black and white photographs, will appeal to a wide range of readers.

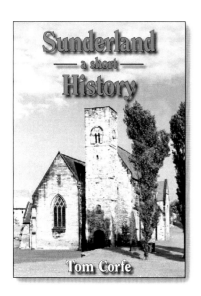

Sunderland – a Short History is an evocative account of Sunderland's past that traces the story of human activity on Wearside from prehistoric times with an appealing blend of scholarship, affection and lucidity. The book first appeared in 1973 and is one of the finest contributions ever made to the literature on Sunderland.